MCDONNELL F3H DE

DEMONOLOGY

PHOTO ABOVE — Very clean natural metal XF3H-1, 125444, in flight. Note partially open nose gear door and open auxillarly engine air intake on the fuselage side, also note absence of afterburnner on derated engine. MDC photo.

INTRODUCTION

Anyone having photos or other information on this aircraft or other 50's era naval aircraft, may submit them for possible inclusion in future issues. Any material submitted will become the property of NAVAL FIGHTERS unless prior arrangement is made. Individuals are responsible for security clearance of any material before submission. **ISBN 0-942612-12-4**

S. Ginter, 1754 Warfield Cir., Simi Valley, California 93063.

All rights reserved. No part of this publication may be reproduced, stored in a retrieval system, or transmitted in any form by any means electronic, mechanical or otherwise without the written permission of the publisher.
© **1985**   *Steve Ginter*

DEVELOPMENT

The McDonnell F3H Demon is probably the least remembered modern Naval fighter, even though it was our first true all-weather missile fighter. When the weather prevented the agile F8U, F4D and F11F from flying, the Demon could still be launched. A glamorous plane the Demon was not, primarily due to its lack of performance. The F3H remained underpowered throughout its career, so much so that it was tagged by fleet pilots as the "lead sled".

ENGINE PROBLEMS

When the invitations to bid were issued in May of 1948, the Demon was to be anything but underpowered. The F3H along with its runner-up the Douglas F4D Skyray were to be powered by the Navy's newest, highest thrust jet engine, the Westinghouse J40. This engine promised aobut twice the thrust of jet engines then in navy service. The XF3H-1 prototypes were ordered in Jan. of 1949, but did not fly until 7 Aug. 1951. This delay was due primarily to the unavailability of the J40 engine. The original engine was to be a Westinghouse J40-WE-8, but was changed to a J40-WE-10, and then a J40-WE-6 non-afterburning engine was detailed to be used temporarily till either the WE-8 or WE-10 would be available for testing. Continued problems with the J40 caused McDonnell to notify the Navy in July of 1951 that possibly another engine should be picked as it appeared the J-40 might not be available. As testing continued, it became evident that the higher powered WE-10 was in trouble and a production version of the WE-8 called a WE-22 was ordered for the initial production machines. In Jan. 1952 the second XF3H-1, 125445, flew, and in

PHOTOS — Four ground views of XF3H-1, 125444, taken on July 6, 1951 at McDonnell's St. Louis plant. Pilot is getting ready for taxi tests. MDC photos. Note the nose high attitude of the prototype, production aircraft used a shorter nose gear to help improve visibility.

RECOMMENDED DEMON READING

Aeroplane Monthly, March 1978, F3H Demon by Hal Andrews. Air Fan, Jan. - Feb. 1983, F3H Demon by Stephane Nicolaou. Proceedings, April 1982, Demon by Captain J. O'Rourke USN

CONTRIBUTORS

ROGER BESECKER, HENRY BLECHA, ROBERT BROADUS, JIM BURRIDGE, CAL CALLAWAY, E.J. CREAGER, R.W. DOWNEY, CAPT. DREESEN, HARRY GANN, STEVE GINSBERG, "MULE" HOLMBERG, CLAY JANSSON, R.C. KOEHNEN, LEO KOHN, BOB KOWALSKI, GORDON LABERT, WILLIAM LARKINS, ROBERT LAWSON, McDONNELL, DAVE MENARD, LCDR. HARRY MILNER, COL. MILLER, S. NICOLAOV, EV PAYETTE, RON PICCIANI, ROBERT PUKALA, MICK ROTHE, WILLIAM SWISHER, TOMY THOMASON, NICK WILLIAMS and STAN WYKOFF.

PHOTO ABOVE — Rollout publicity photo of 125445 with a Naval Reserve FH-1 Phantom from NAS Birmingham and a factory fresh F2H-3 Banshee in the background. Note the XF2H-1 still has the protective paper over the canopy. MDC photo.

PHOTO BELOW — The second XF3H-1 is launched from the deck of the USS Coral Sea (CVA-43) in Oct. 1953 during carrier suitability tests which demonstrated the insufficient power that was provided by the J40 engine. National Archives photo.

April McDonnell strongly suggested that the WE-22 engines be replaced by the Allison J71 with afterburner. In Jan. 1953, the first flight of the WE-8 engined Demon took place. Flight testing proved the WE-8 to be inadequate, and the decision was made to equip two F3H-1s with J71 engines. From here it was concluded that the 61st and subsequent F3H should be equipped with the J71. Continued J-40-WE-22 problems finally led to a modified engine designated a WE-22A. In Aug. carrier suitability trials began, but were not completed until late Oct. due to engine problems. This was followed by the first flight of the J-40 equipped F3H-1N, 133489, on 24 Dec. 1953. As testing continued, XF3H-1 125444 was lost when the McDonnell test pilot ejected following a fuel explosion. This was the second engine failure in 125444, the first was on 2 Aug. 1952 when turbine failure caused her to land short of the runway. Later in March of 1954 a F3H-1N was abandoned at NATC after a complete engine failure. After this, all F3H's were grounded for over three months for engine fixes. The first flight of a J71 engined F3H-1N, 133519, occurred in late Oct. 1954 and the first flight of the J71 equipped F3H-2N, 133520, took place on 11 Jan. 1955. Jan. 1955 would also see the successful completion of Navy J71 evaluations, as well as the second J71 prototype, 133521, taking to the air. In Feb. 1954 during BIS trials, continued J40 engine failures grounded all of the J40 engined Demons. J40 flying was resumed in April, but continued engine failures and two engine accidents led to the total grounding of all J40 F3H's on 7 July 1955. The brand new Demons at St. Louis were barged down the Mississippi River to be used as training aids and monuments. This river journey led to a congressional investigation.

AIRFRAME DEVELOPMENT

Of the 56 F3H-1s, 25 never flew and there were 8 major accidents; three due directly to engine failures, three involving the aircraft or its equipment, 2 for unknown causes.

When the J-40 project was dropped, $91 million had been spent on the F3H-1N. $82 million went to McDonnell, $300,000 to Goodyear, $9 million to Temco and $107 million to Westinghouse for the J-40 engine program. Westinghouse was implicitly declared responsible for the disaster and quit the engine business a few months later.

The end came for the J-40 Demon with 21 of the F3H-1s being designated as mechanics training aids or as structural and armament test craft. The remaining 29 F3H-1s were to be re-engined with the Allison J-71.

From here the J71 was developed into the Demons powerplant, however it never did produce all the needed power to push the Demon around the skies in typical fighter pilot style.

In July 1949 the XF3H-1 mock-up inspection was held at the McDonnell plant in St. Louis. The only major gripe was engine accessability. Steps to correct this gripe as well as weight cutting measures were taken. The major weight reductions were manifested in minimum forward armor protection for the cockpit and the change from power to manual folding wing. Oct. was to be the date of the next inspection, but in Sept. engine changes added 13 in. and 500 lbs. to the airframe. These changes pushed the projected first flight date back to April 1951. In 1950 it was discovered that the nose gear was not strong enough, so a complete redesign was initiated, causing another 150 lbs. increase in weight. Also about this time the radome was redesigned and on Aug. 9 and 10 the mock-up reinspection occurred. The inspection resulted in a return to the power-folded wings. In early 1951 a change in requirements to an all-weather general purpose fighter caused a great increase in fuselage fuel requirements and thus a general fattening of fuselage lines and an increase in weight. Finally in July 1951 the XF3H-1 conducted taxi tests and then flew on 7 Aug. 1951.

Because of pressures of the Korean war, aircraft production progressed during prototype testing. The first production Demons were to be labeled F3H-1Ns. The first major change from the prototype came when the entire nose section including the cockpit, was tilted down 5° to increase the pilots visibility. an interesting feature of the early Demons was a one-piece windshield that appeared on the F3H-1Ns and early 2Ns. In Feb. 1955 these windshields were replaced by a conventional three-piece design. this was done because it was believed that failure of the single-piece windshield had caused an accident.

Wing changes that occurred were the addition of mid-span ailerons in Jan. 1952, and the addition of a 40 in. extension to the trailing edge at the root in Oct. 1952. This extension caused the wing to form a straight line from the fuselage to the wing tip, and a 17% increase in wing area. The final wing changes came in 1956. A wing twisting problem was corrected by installing inboard spoilers. The last major change to the appearance of the Demon came in 1957 when the flat-topped "beaver tail" was replaced by a shorter, tapered tail cone.

Initially the Demon was to have been equipped with the APQ-50 radar, but this was replaced by the APG-51A.

FLIGHT TESTING THE F3H-1

Captain Dreesen flew most of the Navy's second generation of jet fighters while assigned to NATC Patuxent River in the early 1950's. (See Naval Fighters Number Six for his account of test flying the Cutlass and Number Ten for his experiences with the FJ-2.)

Dreesen described the F3H-1 flight test program at Pax River as "sort of a joke," because everyone knew that it would have to be re-engined and that the Navy would never use it. "We were just flying it to prepare for the real airplane, the F3H-2. The J-40 engine was

7

PHOTOS: AT LEFT — Two views of prototype F3H-1N, 133489, undergoing construction. THIS PAGE, TOP – Takeoff of prototype F3H-1N, 133489, on Dec. 31, 1953. BELOW – Two flight views of 133489, on the same date, note white area under horizontal tail. This was the first Demon delivered to the Navy. MDC photos.

8

PHOTOS: ABOVE — F3H-1N, 133491, at Dayton, Ohio, in Sept. 1954, note starter cart which this Demon carried with it, ship is overall blue with natural metal leading edges and landing gears. Photo via W.T. Larkins. BELOW – Rejected F3H-1N Demons await their fate at McDonnell's St. Louis plant after their permanent grounding. 9-26-55 photo via S. Nicolaou.

unreliable in every respect and it was a shame. Although the airplane was big and heavy, it was very maneuverable, very comfortable, and in many ways a lovely airplane to fly. I suspect that if it had had a better engine than the J-71 with which it ended up, it might really have been a long-term Fleet aircraft."

Unfortunately the F3H had been designed around the J-40, and when it turned out to be a disaster the Navy simply had to go hunting for engines. The J-40 was supposed to have delivered 10-11,000 lbs. thrust, about 15,000 with afterburner. It barely produced 11,000 with afterburner. The F4D and the A3D had also been designed around the J-40, and they got the J-57. It was realistically the only alterntive for them, but using it entailed delays, because the Air Force had at that time pretty much tied up the entire J-57 production line. Production was increased to accommodate the Navy, and the switch on the A3D was fairly simple since the engines were in pods. But the F4D and the F3H had been designed with bifurcated ducts specifically for the pressure patterns

the front end of the J-40 engine was supposed to produce. Substituting engines required redesigning the ducts, but only so much could be done without redesigning the entire aircraft, which was not acceptable. For the F4D, it meant that the J-57 produced 600-800 lbs. less thrust than it did in aircraft which had been designed to accept it."

Dreesen and four or five other pilots assigned to Armament Test at the Naval Air Test Center each got about six hops in the F3H-1. Of the sixty F3H-1's produced, changes were made in the second batch of thirty that allowed them to be fitted with the J-71. It would have been too expensive to bring the first thirty up to J-71 standards, so they were sent to Pax River and to some training squadrons. "The Bureau of Aeronautics thought it was a sensible way for people to get experience on a new airplane, but apparently they weren't paying too much attention to the airplane. At Patuxent in particular, everyone was having engine failures, engine overtemperature situations, overtemperatures in the turbine systems. Fortunately there were no real crashes in each case the pilot was able to get the airplane back on the ground."

Dreesen described the F3H-1's performance as "farcical." the miserable performance of the J-40 required very long takeoff runs. "The only way to get the airplane going really fast was to get up to about 35,000 feet, go into burner for a while, and then dive. It would go supersonic very easily, as long as it was going straight down. It was a smooth, neat aircraft, but the engine was worthless. It was very easy in slow-speed flight at altitutde for the pilot to get behind the power curve. In that situation the only way you could recover or to pick up speed was to drop the nose. Even going into afterburner would still leave you behind the power curve. If you let it get too slow at high altitude nothing would accelerate it except diving. The same thing was true in the landing configuration. It had nice, smooth slow-speed flight, but if you were in slow-speed flight on landing and lifted the nose too high, it would continue to declerate under full power. Although we joked about being the only living F3H-1 pilots, none of us had any real problems because we knew all this before we went into the flight program. As I remember, McDonnell had a couple of pilots killed during their test program—engine failures. We knew it was just an interim aircraft, so we flew it very carefully, and in Armament Test as least, we had no problems."

Finally the Bureau of Aeronautics decided to ground the F3H-1. In spite of all the problems with the engines, the dash-ones at Armament Test were the only ones in the Navy that reached thirty hours of flight time with the original engines. In fact, they were undergoing the thirty-hour engine checks when the grounding order was issued. It was decided that they would be given to the maintenance schools for trainees to practice bending metal and pulling wire on. Pax River's F3H-1's were to be put on a barge for transport to Norfolk where they would be put on flatcars and taken to Memphis and other training installations. The Armament Test director, described by Dreesen as "mildly fiesty," sent a special message to BuAer in which he pointed out that his was the only organization in the Navy to have gotten the F3H-1 through thirty hours of flight time with the original engines. Therefore, he concluded, they should be allowed to fly them to the training bases instead of ignominiously loading them on a barge. BuAer didn't see it that way, and they departed Pax River by barge.

According to Dreesen, "the Westinghouse engine failures ruined an entire generation of Naval aircraft, with the exception of the A3. Both the F7U and F3H were potentially competititve with the Air Force's Century Series fighters, had their original engines performed up to design specifications. The combination of delayed deliveries and degraded performance caused by major engine changes in established basic designs rendered them relatively ineffectual aircraft when finally delivered. This generation of Navy fighter aircraft the F3H, the F4D and the F7U was essentially destroyed by Westinghouse."

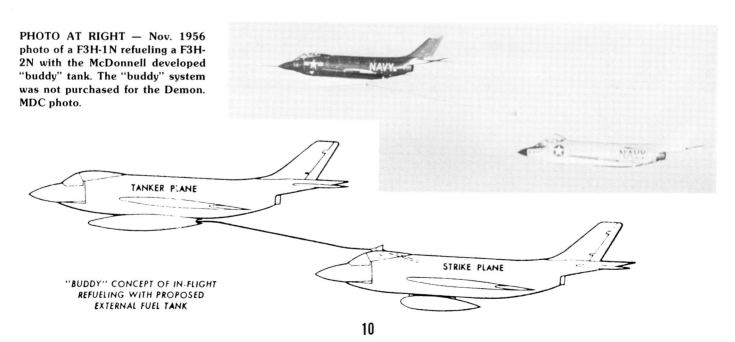

PHOTO AT RIGHT — Nov. 1956 photo of a F3H-1N refueling a F3H-2N with the McDonnell developed "buddy" tank. The "buddy" system was not purchased for the Demon. MDC photo.

"BUDDY" CONCEPT OF IN-FLIGHT REFUELING WITH PROPOSED EXTERNAL FUEL TANK

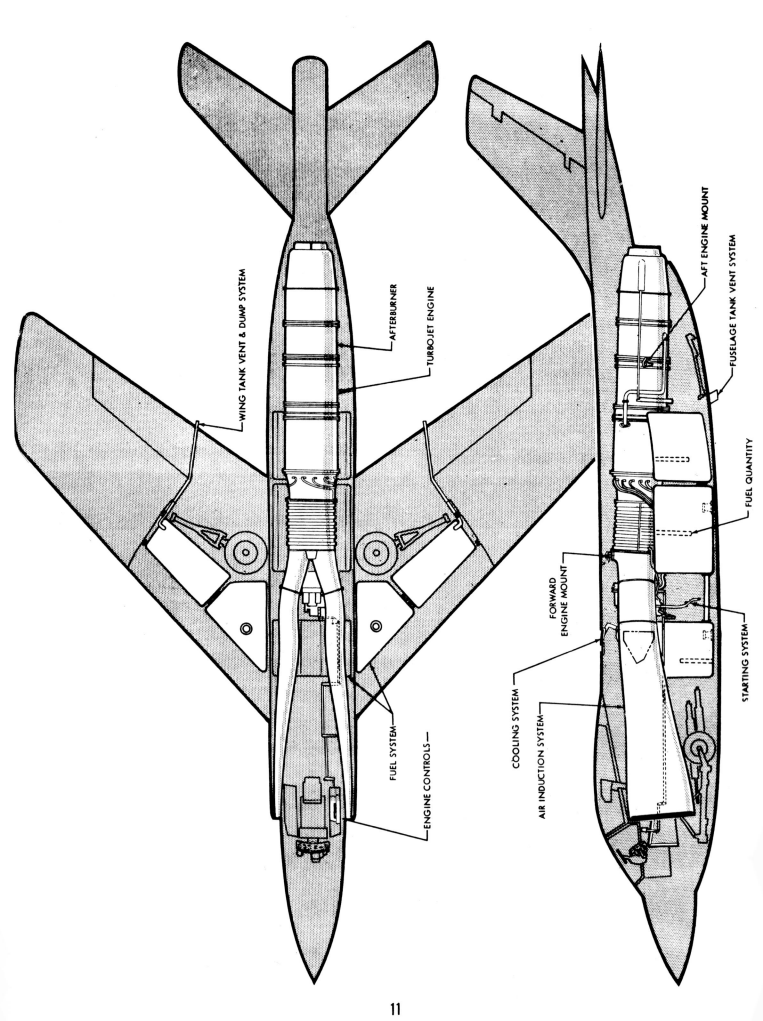

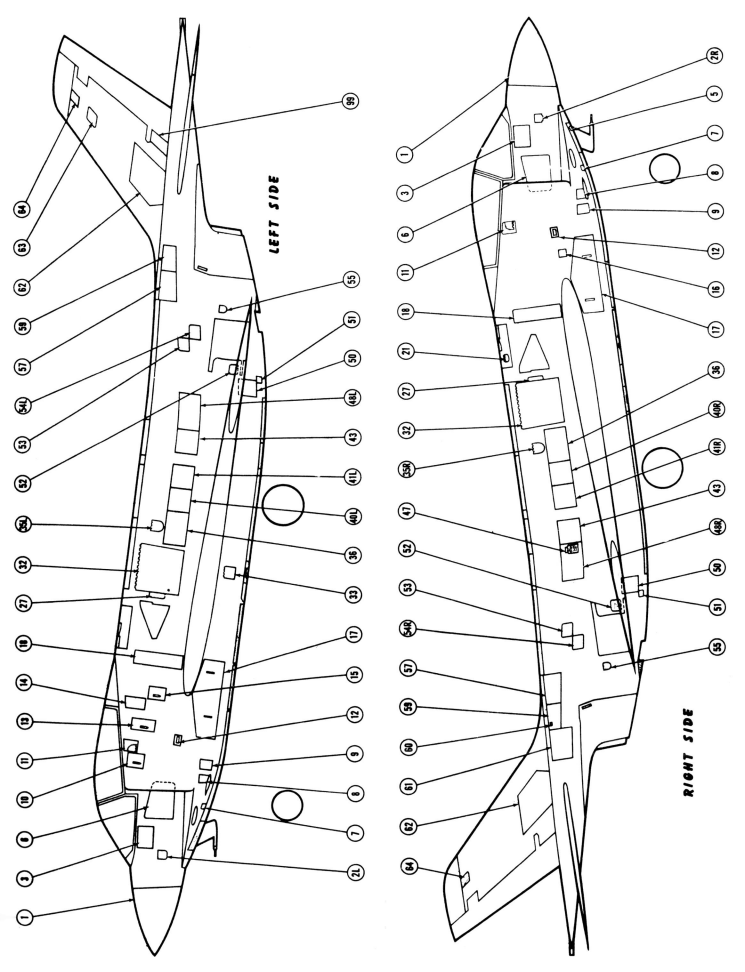

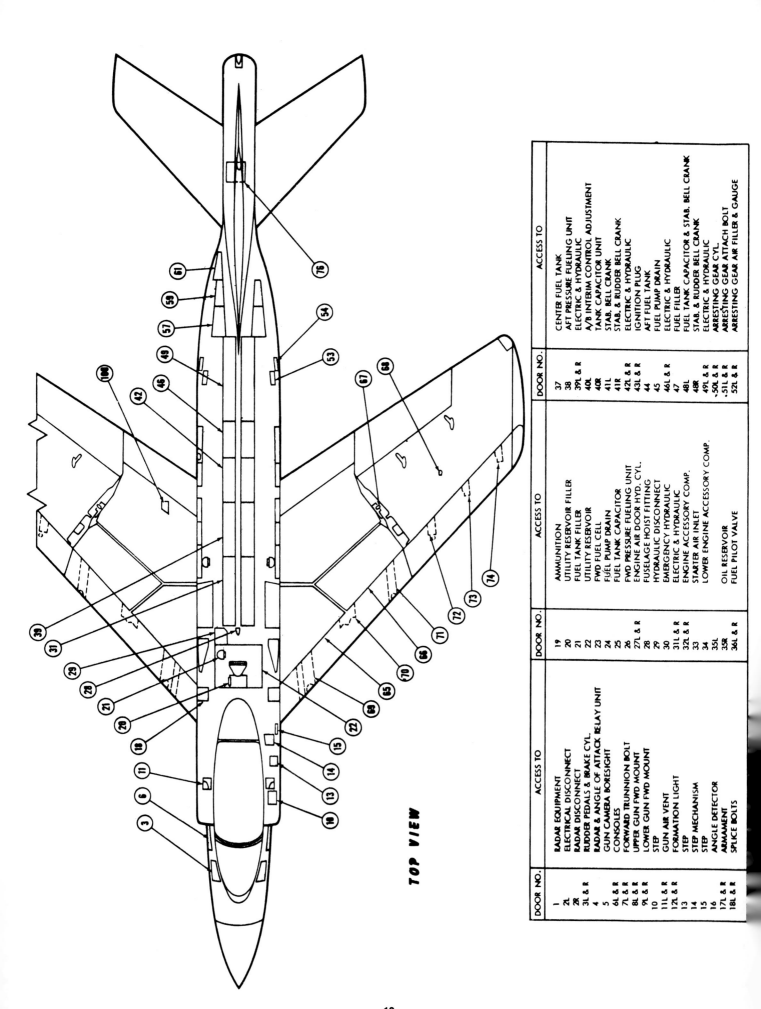

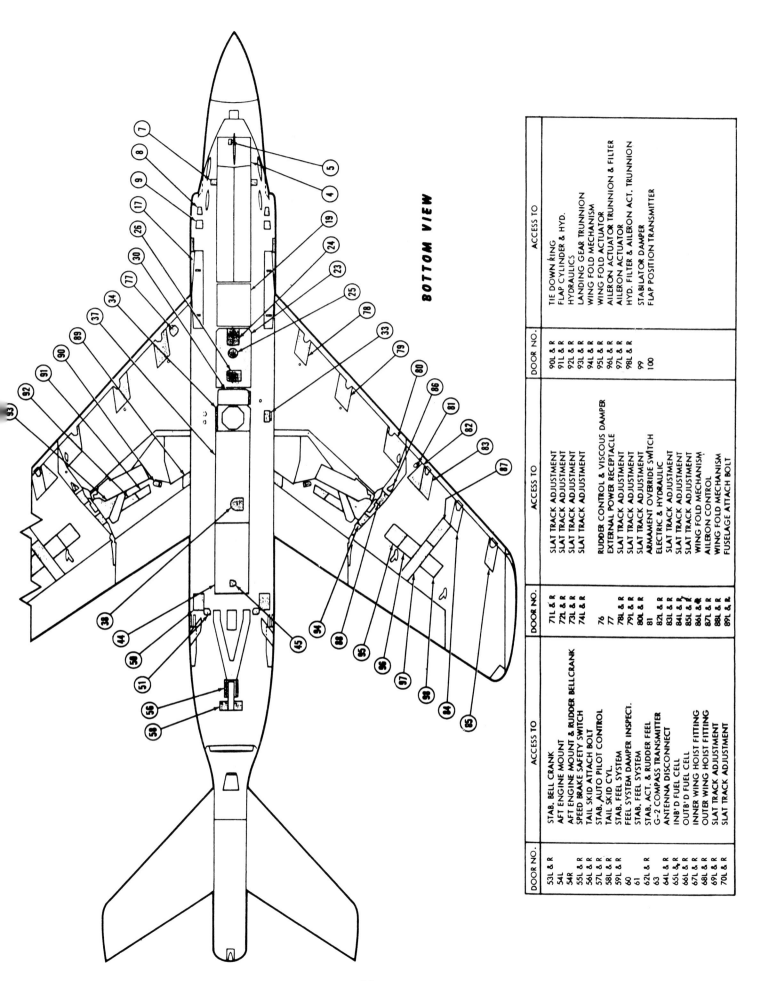

PHOTOS: AT LEFT, TOP — Comparison study of a F3H-1N and a F3H-2N. Note the greater wing area of the 2N. The photo clearly shows the one-piece windscreen of the F3H-1Ns and the early F3H-2Ns as well as the stenciling locations on both aircraft. AT LEFT AND BELOW — Two views of F3H-2N, 133549, on 4-22-55. Note excellent pilot visibility and intake details. Aircraft is gull-grey and white with flat black nose areas and grey test probe. MDC photos. PHOTOS ABOVE — Two views of F3H-2N, 133550, construction #62 on the nose, in flight on 6-16-55. Note the pitot tube on the F3H-2N is on the lower nose section, again note the early one-piece windscreen. The upper photo shows the Demon with its more modern looking stablemate the F-101 Voodoo. MDC photos.

CARRIER SUITABILITY TESTS

Carrier Qualififcaiton tests were conducted for the F3H-2N (133559) the week of 12 Sept. 1955. During this time 23 cat shots and 22 arrested landings were completed. The first tests were completed by CDR. Robert Dose, CO of VX-3. The tests proved successful and the Demon was cleared to start FIP provided McDonnell incorporated some minor improvements during periodic overhauls.

FIP started in Jan. 1956 and was completed by March. It was conducted at the Naval Air Test Center, Patuxent River, Maryland, with three NATC pilots along with pilots from VX-3, VC-3 and VF-14. A total of 608 flight hours were logged, including 142 night hours and 42 instrument hours. FIP testing was completed ahead of schedule and was successful.

The first fleet Demon squadron, VF-14, took delivery of their first aircraft on 7 March 1956. One month later CDR. Stone and VC-3 received their first two F3H-2Ns. VC-3 was responsible for training of West Coast aircrews. VX-3 and VX-4 also received Demons for continued testing.

The Demons operational career lasted some eight and one half years. From 7 March 1956 until 17 Sept. 1964 when VF-161 retired its last "Screaming Demon".

PHOTOS AT RIGHT: TOP — Interesting silhouette photo from below of a "daisy chain", showing a FJ-4B fueling a F3H which is fueling a A4B whos doing another A4B. USN photo. **AT RIGHT BELOW** — F3H-2N, 133572, on 6-4-56 with two belly-tanks and four 2 inch FFAR rocket pods. MDC photo.

F3H CHRONOLOGY

1. Bid, May 1948, XF3H-1.
2. Contract awarded, Sept. 1948 (125444-445).
3. Mock-up inspection, July 1949.
4. Mock-up reinspection, 9 & 10 Aug. 1950.
5. March 1951, order placed for 150 F3H-1.
6. July 1951, 125444 completes taxi tests.
7. Production mock-up inspection 11-13 July 1951.
8. 7 Aug. 1951, first flight XF3H-1, 125444.
9. F3H-1P ordered.
10. F3H-1s ordered.
11. Jan. 1952, XF3H-1 125445 joins flight testing.
12. Jan. 1953, Navy evaluates XF3H-1.
13. June 1953, F3H-1 designation changed to F3H-1N because of approval of the Sparrow I missile-equipped version as the F3H-1M.
14. Aug. 1953, mock-up inspection for J71 engine installation planned for 61st aircraft on.
15. Aug.1953, XF3H-1 125444 assigned carrier trials.
16. Oct. 1953, carrier suitability test completed.
17. Dec. 1953, F3H-1N first flight, 133489.
18. Early 1954, F3H-2N, -2M and -2P ordered, also #31 and #33 F3H-1Ns to serve as J71 test aircraft and #32 and #34 to serve as F3H-2N prototypes.
19. Sept. 1954, first flight of J71 Demon #133519.
20. Oct. 1954, F3H orders cut to 280 and F3H-2Ps deleted.
21. 11 Jan. 1955, first flight F3H-2N prototype #133520.
22. Jan. 1955, J71 prototype 133519 completes evaluation.
23. Jan. 1955, second J71 prototype flys #133521.
24. April 1955, first production F3H-2N flys #133549.
25. May 1955, F3H-2N BIS trials completed.
26. 7 July 1955, all J40 engined Demons grounded and most aircraft scrapped.
27. Sept. 1955, F3H-2N carrier suitability tests started on USS Ticonderoga, CVA-14.
28. Nov. 1955, carrier trials completed.
29. Nov. 1955, Sparrow III equipped Demon authorized and the F3H-2M started flight testing.
30. 3 Jan. 1956, six F3H-2Ns start FIP program at NATC.
31. 7 March 1956, FIP program completed.
32. April 1956, deliveries to VF-14 started.
33. Sept. 1956, F3H-2 in flight testing.
34. 1956, orders placed for first 90 then an additional 149 Demons.
35. 1957, first Demon squadrons deployed and F3H-2 completed BIS trials.
36. Nov. 1959, production completed.
37. 1962, F3H-2 became F-3B and F3H-2M became F-3C.
38. Sep. 1964, the Demon was retired from last squadron VF-161.

Two good underside views of F3H-2N, 133572, in June 1956. Note stencil and antenae locations. MDC photos.

F3H-2M

Early on in its development the basic concept of the Demon was changed to missile interceptor. Enter the F3H-2M (F3C after 1962) which would carry and test the Sparrow I and III systems and the AAM-N-7 Sidewinder weapon systems.

The first production F3H-2M arrived at the Naval Air Missile Test Center, Point Mugu, Calif. on 10 Feb. 1956. The first deliveries to operational units occurred in Sept. 1956 to the "Jolly Rogers" of VF-61 and the "Top Hatters" of VF-14.

Once the Sparrow III system became operational the Sparrow III aircraft were designated F3H-2s. Even F3H-2N aircraft were modified by the squadrons and VX-4 into the F3H-2 configuration.

PHOTOS: ABOVE — F3H-2N, construction #213, with three-piece windscreen takes off from St. Louis. Photo via Don Spering / A.I.R. MIDDLE — Early F3H-2M, 133569, construction #81, armed with dark blue Sparrow I missiles. Photo via Don Spering / A.I.R. BOTTOM — F3H-2M, 137037, construction #156, in flight with Sparrow I missiles on 10-4-1956. MDC photo.

PHOTOS: TOP — F3H-2N, 137007, construction #200 on 1-23-57, with the new Sparrow III missiles mounted on the wings. Missiles are blue and white with beige nose cones. MDC photo. MIDDLE — Same aircraft in 1958 with day-glo red tail. Bowers photo via W.T. Larkins. BOTTOM — F3H-2N, 137029, 1958, with six 500 lb. bombs and two 2,000 lb. bombs mounted. Bowers photo via W.T. Larkins.

. . . PRACTICALLY LANDS ITSELF

THE DEMON

As RECALLED BY LCDR HARRY MILNER USN RET.

EDITORS NOTE LCDR Milner had a long association with the Demon, starting in 1957 with the first Demon squadron, VF-14, and ending with the last F3H squadron, VF-161, in 1964. He flew Demons with VF-14, VF-101, VF-151, VF-121 and VF-161. He finally timed out with 1,300 hours in the Demon.

More than most aircraft I would say the Demon was a learning experience, and the more you learned about it the more you liked it. We used to say there were two kinds of Demon Drivers, those who were dead and those who loved the airplane. The F3H had a super Cadillac ride that made a Phantom look squirrelly by comparison. What the Demon really needed was an engine. If we could have had a Phantoms J-79 we would have had an airplane that would of really watered some eyes. The J-79 would have reduced the weight and size of the engine and allowed us to carry more onboard fuel; as well as giving us a very favorable thrust to weight ratio. Even though handicapped by its powerplant, the F3H was a strong, dependable, safe, reliable and efficient all weather missile fighter. Its radar allowed it to fly and carry out its mission of fleet defense when all other fighters were grounded by the weather.

My proof that the Demon was an excellent aircraft is the fact that only one squadron has ever won the coveted combination Battle "E" and Safety award three years in a row, and that was VF-14 in 1959-60 and 61. Interestingly enougt it was done in the only airplane that both the manufacturer and the Navy would rather not talk about. Most people who weren't directly involved with the aircraft would like to forget it even existed; in fact, I heard a rumor that daddy Mac. had sued a model maker in the 50's for trying to issue a kit of the Demon.

My first contact with the Demon came in Dec. 1955 while I was undergoing flight training at NAS Pensacola, Florida. There were about a dozen of the all blue F3H-1s parked along the sea wall (fate unknown). These aircraft had been barged down the Mississippi River from Mcdonnell's St. Louis plant after it was determined that they were too underpowered for the Navys requirements. the F3H-1 differed visibly from the F3H-2 in having a smaller nose and in the absence of the characteristic swing belly. My first impression of the blue F3H-1 was that of a praying mantis, and at that point, what with their reputation and such, I hoped I would not get involved with the Demon.

The next time I saw a Demon was when I was at Key West going through FAWTUATLANT (Fleet All Weather Training Unit Atlantic) Detachment A in July of 1957. We were riding in the right seat of the F3D Skyknight while learning the fine art of radar intercepts in preparation for joining an all weather fighter squadron. This was before the days of the RAG, when each squadron was responsible for training its own pilots in type. In fact, there was no such thing as a Natops manual, just a pilots handbook.

When I arrived at my first squadron, VF-14, we had fourteen aircraft, only one of which was in an "up" condition, and nobody in the squadron had been checked out in the F3H. All told there were nineteen pilots in the squadron, including the CO, CDR Martin "Butch" O'Neil, and the XO, LCDR. Art Adams. Butch had a well thought out idea of how a RAG should work and tried to implement his ideas in our training. We got a lot of hands on experience before our first flights, as most of our aircraft were in pieces. In fact one had been so cannibalized that it had to be barged and trucked to Cecil Field, Florida.

My introduction to the Demon finally came when the Skipper borrowed three F3H pilots to show us the ropes. First we learned to start and stop her, then start-taxi and shut down, and then first flight. It was Feb of 1958 when I first took the duty runway in my trusty Demon. I hadn't put much thought into the fact that I hadn't been alone in an aircraft since May of 1957 and that was in a straight winged F9F-2 Panther. Now I was all set to go in an afterburning, smoke-blowing, swing-bellied Demon, so it was hit the AB and go for it. It was a real thrill as I finally caught myself going through 40,000 ft.

ENTERING THE COCKPIT

The first thing that would attract your attention as a new Demon pilot was the fact that you had to be a mountain goat to get into the cockpit, as it was some thirteen feet above the deck. Aboard ship, we at first had a cumbersome ladder that folded in the middle and was a real bear in the wind. It was replaced by a single piece non-folding tubular ladder that floated. We used these new ladders for a short period of time till the sailors had managed to throw them all over the side. The first time a sailor pitched one over the side and got caught, he laughed and said, "what are you going to do with evidence?" He then turned around and saw it floating in the ships wake. So, generally, we didn't use the ladders.

The way we normally entered the cockpit was to scale up to it. the speed brakes would ususally bleed open so it was one foot in the speed brake one in the flap and up the wing to the three goat steps that stuck out of the side of the fuselage. You would step across the goat steps to climb into the cokpit while holding onto the canopy bottom rail. The goat step started out being something the size of your finger and developed into a "L" shaped hook with a non-skid surface. We also added a big drawer puller handle on the back of the canopy to make it considerably safer. Before doing this we lost a gent one night who fell onto the deck and broke his leg pelvis arm and who knows what else. Since these modifications still wouldn't prevent you from sliding off the wing, we installed a non-skid wing-walk. However, we didn't use the regular aircraft type, but the type found on ships ladders.

Once into the cockpit a new pilot would realize he had a considerble amount of room. It was larger than a Phantoms cockpit and you certainly had a lot better visibility. The visibility was incredible. It gave me the feeling that if I leaned forward and looked down that I would see the nosewheel. You couldn't but you could see someone standing next to the nosewheel. It sure was nice not to have to roll the airplane to see something below you. The rest of your bisibility was restricted normally by the seat and its ledges.

APG-51 RADAR SYSTEM

The next thing that would grab a new pilots attention would be the second grip behind the throttle. This was the radar control stick. In the early days, it was a real Rube Goldberg type of thing. the stick had a switch on top that was a two speed "gate" switch. The choices being in and out. With this system you just couldn't superimpose the range gate over a target very easily. It moved either way too fast or way too slow. So we changed the control so that the top was an antenna elevation switch. The movement of the handle back and forth became the range gate in and out. This made the whole thing a whole lot smoother and is basically what we find in the F-4 and F-14 today. In reality the hand control we use now was developed in the Demon, although its been modified since then.

Another development we introduced was nadar. With this capability a tape of the entire attack presentation on the radar could be made for post-flight review. We could then get a tape from lock-on to missile firing that we would play on television type gear.

Another feature we instituted was an antenna "L" marker, which would move from the right side of the scope to the left while at max-range and left to right while at mid-range. From this you could tell what the intercept geometry was and of course you'd have range and rate circles and the gyro indication on the scope. The Demons radar display changed from a simple system to the more complex system with collapsing range circles, etc. that's found in the F4 Phantom today. The Demon's set had some capabilities built into it that were really unique. One of these features was a mapping mode which encorporated a range expanding mode within that mapping. The map scale went out to 200 miles and you had a bracket you could run in and out with a twistable knob. If you pulled that knob up, the entire scope beccame a 20 mile square. This would enable you to blow up a target when still 180 miles out. This gave us the ability to pick up RB-66 aircraft at a range of 180 miles during WESIG 1959 (WEAPONS SYSTEMS EVALUATION GROUP EXERCISE), during a jamming evoulation against the ship. The radar ranges as I recall were from top to bottom of the scope, 30 miles in the normal presentation which could be enlarged to about eight miles.

As originally built, lock-on could only be accomplished when the target was within 15 miles. Luckily, we had some technicians with us who were able to remove the block and allow the radar to operate at its own limitations. So your ability to lock-on was dependent on the size and range of the target and the quality of the return. We were able to obtain lock-ons at just inside 23 miles. This feat was certainly nothing compared to todays F-14s — enviable in comparison with early F-4 Phantoms — incredible when compared with F-8 Crusaders, F4D Skyrays and F3D Skynights.

AUTOPILOT

The next pilot comfort item was the autopilot. The control box was on the starboard console and had a joy stick of its own. It had a couple of function hold buttons, mach and altitude. These enabled you to either hold your mach or your altitude. While the aircraft was in autopilot, you could control it through the use of its little joystick. The system had the capability of controlling the pitch without using the stick, this was done with a knurled knob.

The autopilot itself could be engaged at anytime. If you engaged it in an attitude that exceeded the autopilots hold capability, the aircraft would roll in the reverse of the way it rolled going into the maneuver and recover straight and level. But if you engaged the autopilot within its hold capability limits, you could hold the aircraft in that attitutde.

The autopilot had its own gyro (as did the radar). If you found yourself in an extreme condition of vertigo, you could reach over and engage the autopilot, which would hold you if the aircraft was in a safe attitude. Once held, if you just distrubed the stick on the autopilot, the aircraft would recover to straight and level trimmed flight. As an example, you could roll the plane upside down - nose high - 15° above the horizon, and let it run out of airspeed, then punch in the autopilot and it would roll in the opposite direction - recover - drop the nose - pick up the 200 or 300 kts. you had trimmed for and off you went.

UNSPINNABLE

The Demon was the original unspinnable aircraft. The story here says the MacDonnell test pilot went out to test the Demons spin recovery capabilities. Eight attempts and three hops later, he still was unsuccessful. Finally he pulled a combination maneuver which succeeded in getting the F3H into a spin. He then tried the three known recovery techniques, all of which didn't work. By this time he had passed through 10,000 feet and had deployed the anti-spin chute, which didn't work either. He then attempted to burn off the chute by use of afterburner, and when that failed he ejected. After he had left the aircraft, the Demon recovered while in AB and climbed up through 40,000 ft. while departing the St. Louis area. The airplane flamed out at 40,000 ft. and made its own dead stick landing in a farmers field. It probablly would have been undamaged except that it caught a wingtip during slide out. The outcome of this whole incident was that if you wanted the aircraft to do something weird, you had to hold the controls there, but to recover all you had to do was let go of the stick and rudders.

An interesting side note is that the Air Defense Command was contacted and asked to intercept. When they found out what it was and that it was in AB at

40,000 ft., they said to forget it because they couldn't catch it.

CONTROL SURFACES

The F3H had absolutely incredible rudder and stabilator (flying tail) authority. Directional control on the runway became effective at 20 m.p.h. with use of the rudder. Stabilator control was so good that you could actually compress the nose strut down all the way by pushing the stick forward. On a carrier deck you could even jump the nose wheel off the deck by pushing the stick full forward and full back a couple of times. In fact the wind down the deck was enough for you to be able to swing the nose just through the use of the rudder, which is a real feat considering the Demon did not have a stearable nose wheel.

The other part of our control system was the combination spoiler aileron. The spoiler was set inboard on the top of the wing. These were 1/2 inch aluminum planks that slammed down on top of the wing when you operated them. Our method of trimming stick center at night was to trim the spoilers first. This was done because the spoilers were the only mechanical surface, and if you trimmed them first and then were unable to trim the ailerons level, you knew that your autopilot actuator for the displaced aileron was bad. The aircraft would also switch from aileron to spoiler control automatically somewhere around mach .82 or so.

ARMAMENT

Although four 20mm guns were installed, the Demon evolved into basically an all missile interceptor. In June of 1958, VF-14 took six Demons out to NAS Point Mugu, Calif. The purpose of this cross country was to finish the installation of the Sparrow III systems. The planes were F3H-2N's, which were entirely Sidewinder and gun capable. (The F3H-2Ms, which were Sparrow I capable were never uprated to the Sparrow III system). When we arrived at Pt. Mugu the CW transmitting gear was installed in the nose well to complete the system. This gear made the aircraft slightly nose heavy.

While at Pt. Mugu our belief in the aircraft grew greatly because the Sparrow III was a super weapon. At that time an interceptor was not designed for hasseling, instead you flew wings level, 250 to 300 kts., while pointing your nose right at the enemy. You would let your enemy do the work for you, the faster he flew the sooner you got to shoot and the quicker the intercept was complete. In that time I never saw a Sparrow miss, however I never saw a sidewinder hit, so I was thrilled with the success of the weapons system.

GUNS + OR -

Since we developed into a missile interceptor and were somewhat underpowered, it became common practice to remove the two upper 20mm guns. This would save about 500 lbs for the guns and 50 lbs for the ammo cans. With the upper guns removed you could use that compartment for baggage stowage. In some photos you will notice blank-offs installed in the upper gun positions. The upper guns were removed instead of the lower ones, because the lower guns had more of a blast reflector apparatus which was harder to remove. We had tried removing all four guns, but discovered that the F3H was then much too light in the nose

REFUELING AND DROP TANKS

We didn't carry drop tanks at VF-14 for a couple of very good reasons — range and performance. Two drop tanks hanging side by side on the narrow fuselage stations netted you a loss in range and performance and a whole five more minutes of flight time. One drop tank was somewhat better; it gave you an additional five to ten minutes of flight time with no increase in range. Unlike VF-14, the following squadrons all carried single drop tanks — VF-31, 151 and 161.

In Jan. 1961, I became the second man to attempt to plug a Demon into an AJ Savage tanker. We had been given no instructions on how it was to be done. The XO, LCDR Roy Cornwell, went in first with the slats and flaps up while going down hill at 180 kts. (500 ft. per. min.). The AJ was going flat out and we were dragging our feet. It didn't work and the XO was unable to complete the engagement. So it was up to me to make the next attempt with the slats out. That little maneuver found me looking at the top of the AJ over my canopy rail while in the inverted position. We finally found out that by using the speed brakes in conjunction with more power we could alter our closing speed properly. This procedure gave us a higher power setting and allowed us more maneuverability. Once we became proficient with the AJ, we decided to try our hand at the venerable Able Dog (Skyraider). The AD worked well too.

Since the refueling capabilities of the Demon were an afterthought and therefore externally mounted, it was relatively easy to remove the probe and cover the openings with a blank-off plate. We ususally flew the airplane with the probe off and when on the beach removed the racks and rails too. Besides the obvious drag savings we saved an additional 180 lbs by removing the refueling gear.

THE F3H VERSUS THE F8

We used to have a axiom that said, the fighter pilot that would win was the one who knew the most about the other guys aircraft. Since no one wanted to know anything about the Demon and it was easy to know anything you wnated to know about the F-8 Crusader, we had a distinct advantage.

The F-8s used to have a hammer head stall maneuver to lose interceptors. they would go straight up in burner and then turn around and come straight down when they ran out. Well, we'd wait for them and catch them on the way back and follow them down the hill. That was a real education for F-8 drivers, who weren't knowledgeable about the F3H.

When the heavy underpowered Demon was full of fuel it was no match for a F-8. But if a F3H hasselled a fully fueled and armed F-8 when the Demon had burned down to fighting weight — F-8 beware. At this point the Demon would have the same thrust-to-weight ratio as the Crusader. It was always a real eye-opener to a F-8 pilot to come off the deck on board ship and find a Demon in a low fuel condition wiating for him. The first time they would try and jump us, they would think they were flying a lead sled, because the Demon would turn around and go the other way inside the F-8's gunnery pursuit curve. My favorite maneuver would be to catch a F-8 rolling in and then throw the speed brakes out and slow to 250 kts., and then stash it in burner and put that thing into 90° of bank and just reef it around the corner and meet him head on going the opposite direction flying up his pursuit curve.

I remember encountering another F-8 after carquals off the Florida coast. During carquals we didn't have racks and rails or IFR probes or anything heavy. So one day I had one of these stripped down carqual F3H's out and was playing around when I noticed two F8U-2NEs below me. They were two VF-174 rag birds out practicing intercepts. There was an instructor in the second F-8 who was tagging along with the student at about 38,000 feet. Well I'm sure I destroyed the instructors whole day as I started down on my high side gunnery run from 43,000 feet. You could just see him look out his canopy and say, "a Demon coming down on me — obviously its time for my world famous maneuver", and he stashed it in burner and yanked back on the stick, but instead of going straight up, he just spun out. So while he was doing his octoflugerons while trying to recover the airplane, I casually joined up and flew wing on him. When he recovered and looked out the cockpit and saw me on his wing — you could see the dropped eyelids and gaping open mouth — as if saying how in the world did you do that. He then went through a couple of more gyrations to get rid of me and when that didn't work, he gave up and waved. Once back at the field the instructor, who turned out to be a friend of mine, found me and related how he hadn't know a Demon could do all that.

One of the other things about the maneuverability of the aircraft was that since we had hydraulic control of slats and flaps, we could go slats only, or quarter flaps, or half flaps or whatever. We could go slats only and turn like crazy and if an A-4 Skyhawk tried to match your roll it would end up slipping a slat on the wrong wing and go the other way, particularly if you were slow — which a Demon usually was. We generally stayed in the region of 275 to 300 kts.

SURVIVABILITY

The Demon was a rugged aircraft that had extremely good survival capabilities either ditching, crashing, or even leaving the runway.

The first incident I saw was at Key West, where a F3H left the side of the runway. Since Key West or Boca Chica is at such a low altitiude, it had water on both sides of the runway, and when the plane stopped, the pilot looked over the side and thought he was in the water. So he inflated his Mae West and jumped, but to his shock he found the water only six inches deep.

My roommate, LTJG. "Fab" Fabiszewski, took a Demon into Nice, France with an electrical problem. He came in minus the canopy, gear down, slats down and no flaps. He also was coming in with his nozzle open because his AB mod switch wouldn't work. He came in downwind over the water towards the city. He had actually flamed the aircraft out at 6,000 feet and dived it down to the runway with his ram air driven hydraulic pump spinning from the belly of the plane. He was of course, too fast to stop, so he took it off the side of the runway. Well at Cote D'Azur they used great big river bed rocks on the sides of the runway. He ran across these and finally stopped up against a concrete abutment. All this did was to bend the nose strut.

Another pilot with VF-14, was flying around when he lost AB nozzle control. This gent decided a straight in approach would be best and when he put the gear and flaps down, he couldn't maintain altitude, and found himself settling into the Florida pines. He then picked up his flaps in an attempt to decrease his drag and started plowing pine trees. He then hit AB about the time he hit the ground and continued plowing trees and miraculously got airborne again. He continued into the break and turned downwind to make what he called an uneventful landing minus his main mounts.

Another time a fellow lost his port brake while making an arrested landing. He stood on the right brake to make the airplane stop. This resulted in the nose of his airplane making a half circle which took the tails off of two AD Skyraiders and stopped against a third. About the only damage to the Demon was the destruction of the fiberglass radome and damage to the radar antennae.

One night in the Med, a fellow named Jack Childes was forced to land aboard ship with his port main gear up and locked. On his first pass he caught the #2 wire and the barricade, which stopped him neatly. The Demon Doctors jacked up the airplane, took the main mount out, repaired it, changed the outboard wing panel and we were able to use the aircraft the next day. During my tour with VF-101, I too landed a F3H with the port main mount up, again with minimal damage.

The first stories and photos I ever saw of a Demon in the Florida pines was of a fellow named Ed Feaks who had lost power on take-off and landed wings level while sliding out through the fields. He really tore up some trees, as he went through a farmers field, a fence, a ditch and over a road and down into more trees. When the thing finally came to a halt, the farthest point forward was the seat's stirrups (as his aircraft had been equipped with the McDonnell seat instead of the later Martin Baker seat which didn't have stirrups). So there he sat with a tree right between his knees. Another six inches and his nose would have been touching the tree.

At VF-101 we had a GCA officer by the name of MacElhaney. He was doing some GCA instructor training with a gent named J.C. Barenti. I was walking out to the flightline as the two were coming in.

Mr. Mac was coming down fast behind the trees. As he went behind the trees, I was saying to my students, "Gee I didn't think the runway went that far out." About that time, I saw a big puff of black smoke which marked his point of entry into the water short of the runway. What had happened was that Mr. Mac had been using the blackout bag over his head and when it came to GCA wave off time, it had become entangled with his helmet and he couldn't get it off. He then hit the water and the impact snapped his head forward and the bag came off. After he had waded ashore, the airplane caught fire and burned for the next three days.

AB MOD SWITCH

The Demon had an acceptable rpm range which was pretty limited at full power. As I recall you were supposed to have 99 1/2 to 100 1/2 with a temperature of 677° or "620° and building." Once stabilized and at max military power the nozzle continually hunted to maintian 677°. The nozzle itself was closed hydraulically, but was allowed to open electrically. There was an AC relay that was involved and if it failed, you'd get an open nozzle. With your nozzle in the open position, you just about had enough power in a clean configuration to fly at four or five throusand feet, and when the gear and flaps came down you would come down in a normal glide slope of 4° at landing weight. The AB mod switch was a lift push toggle switch which put the aircraft into after-burner anytime you were above 80% throttle. Since the airplane idled at 76%, it didn't leave you much leeway. Once in burner, the only way out of burner was by turning off the switch.

One time at Key West, a fellow pilot failed to note that his AB mod switch was in AB during his cockpit check. Now since he was an old salt and wanted to show the kids in the rag how to leave the line, he goosed it coming out of the chocks. Of course he went over 80% and the burner lit about the time he applied differential braking, as the Demon did not have a steerable nose wheel. You can well imagine his shock and the few hairy moments until he was able to shut down the burner.

The real purpose of the switch was that if you had a failed open nozzle in flight, and were coming aboard ship, you obviously couldn't be satisfied by the sink rate provided with the gear and flaps down. You needed the power you got at 94-96%. In AB "mod", 84-86% gave you that power, but very slow acceleration.

In the F3H, the curve in the power available range started somewhere around 92%, and more than half your thrust was above that point. Since thats wehre you were when dirty and coming aboard, we frequently used speed brakes because they retracted faster than the power came on. Acceleration time on the engine from idle to military power was like 13 1/2 seconds, and considering idle was about 76%, that just was not a fast engine.

Our type of burner was called a soft lite/open nozzle burner. In this system the nozzle would open and the burner would light. If the nozzle opened and the burner didn't light, you would have an instant loss of power, if it light you'd get a little buck. Now the F-8 Crusader had a J-57 engine which would light with the nozzle closed. This would give you what we called a hard light.

The Demon also had what was called a flat throttle. That is, in the range from 76 to 92%,the throttle would only move about an inch. After that you had about three to three and a half inches to play with. In that three to three and a half inches you were only modulating the engine between 92 and 100%, giving you more finite power control. So you really had to be careful when operating it in the 92% and lower range.

LAST NOTE

Even though the Demon was referred to as a "lead sled", you really could go supersonic if you were straight and level at 8,000 feet. The thing that was nice about the Demons reputation was that if you did bust up someones windows, they would blame a F-8 or F-4

LT. HARRY MILNER

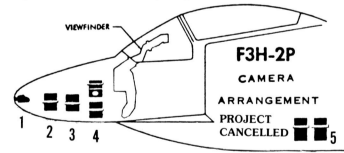

F3H-2P CAMERA ARRANGEMENT PROJECT CANCELLED

FORWARD FIRING	FWD ROTATABLE	AFT ROTATABLE	TRI-METROGON	AFT VERTICAL
1	2	3	4	5
ONE K-25 15" FOCAL LENGTH	ONE CAX-12 3" FOCAL LENGTH	ONE CAX-12 3" FOCAL LENGTH	THREE CAX-12 1 1/2" FOCAL LENGTH	TWO CAX-12 6" FOCAL LENGTH
	OR	OR	OR	OR
	6" FOCAL LENGTH	6" FOCAL LENGTH	TWO CAX-12 6" FOCAL LENGTH	12" FOCAL LENGTH
	OR	OR	OR	OR
	12" FOCAL LENGTH	12" FOCAL LENGTH	ONE CAX-12 12" FOCAL LENGTH	ONE T-11 MAPPING
				OR
				ONE CAS-2a 100 MM STRIP
				OR
				ONE K-17C

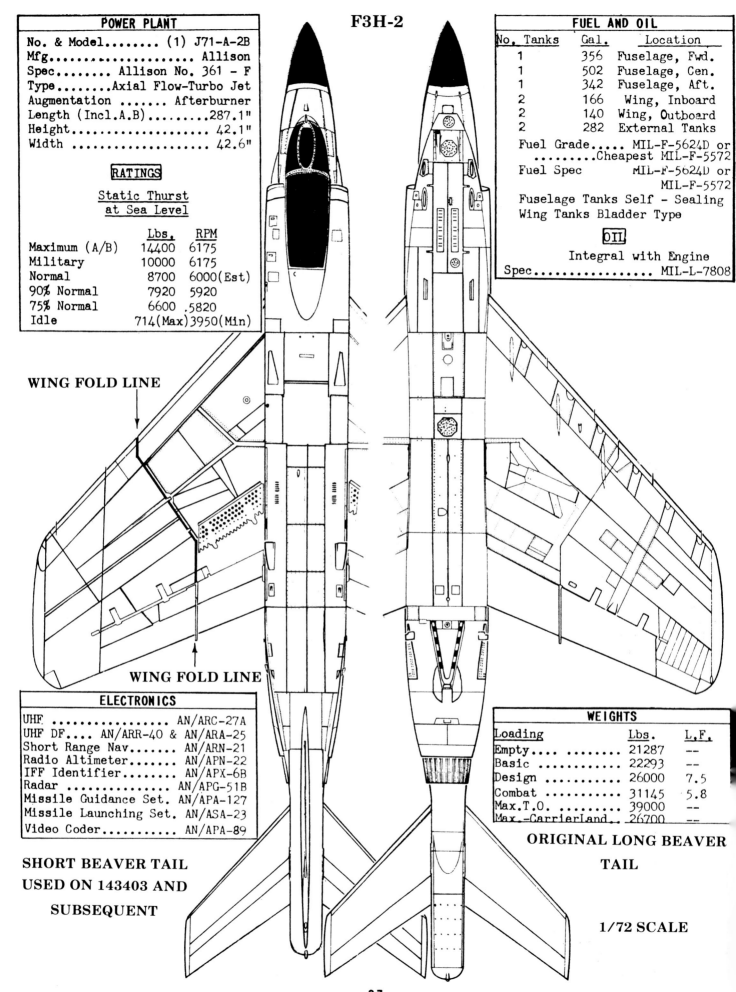

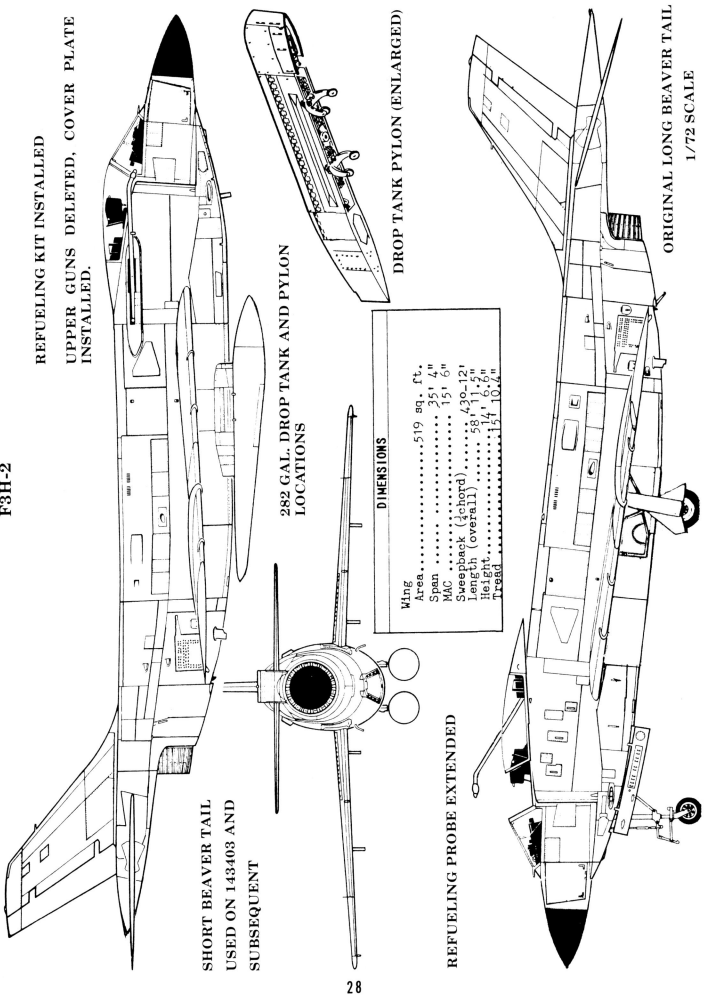

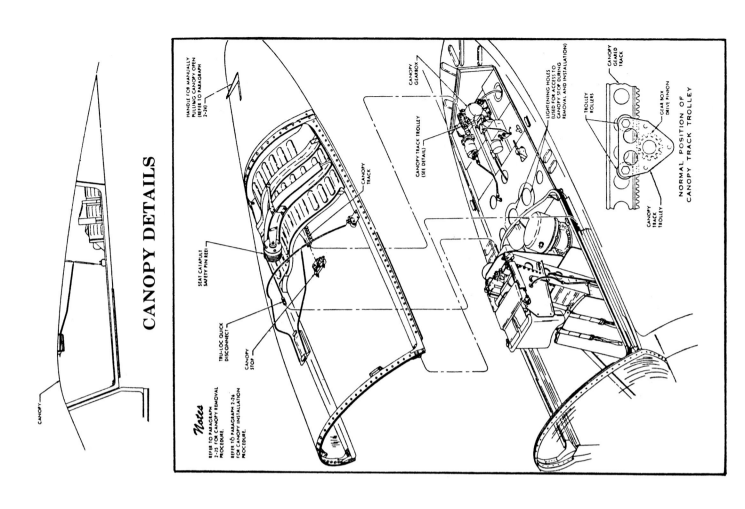

CANOPY DETAILS

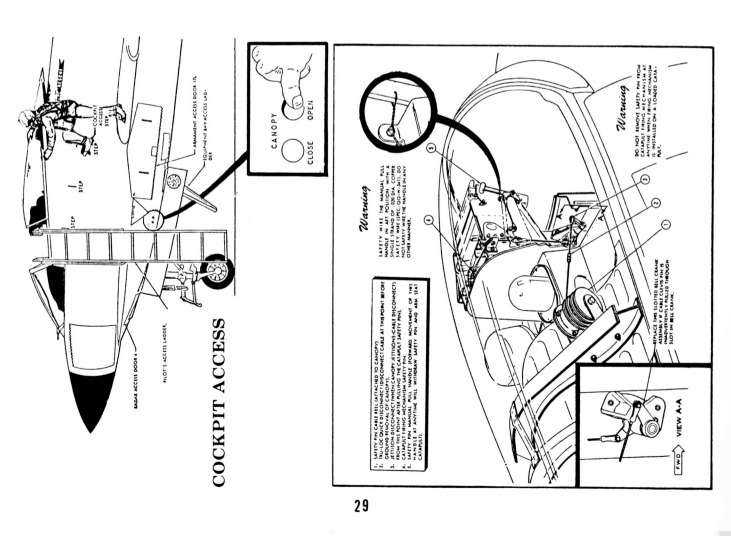

COCKPIT ACCESS

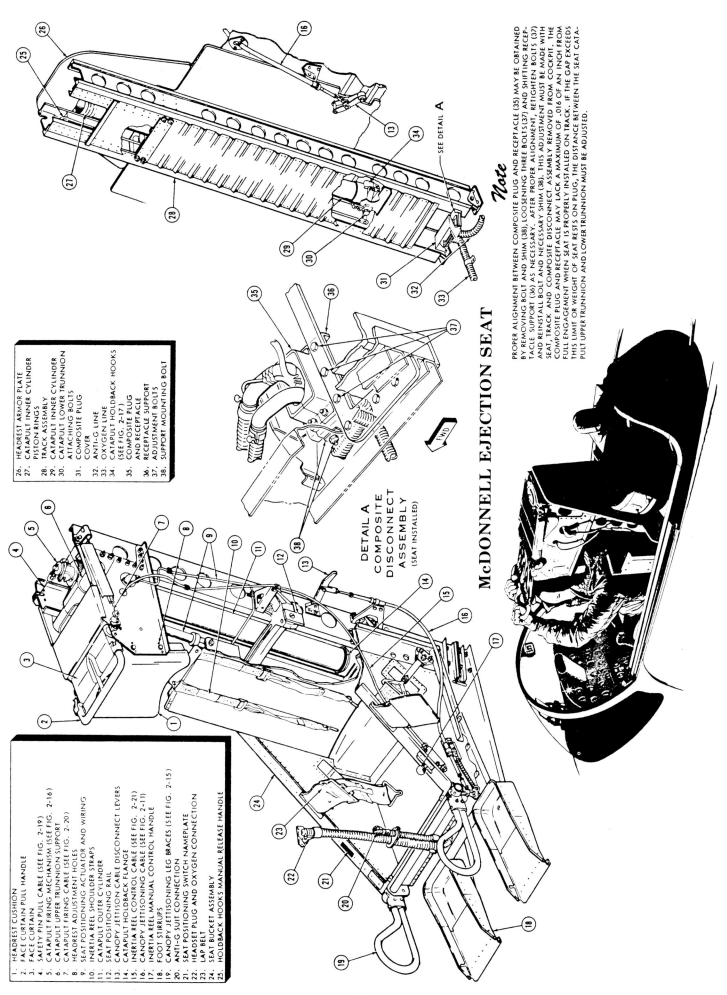

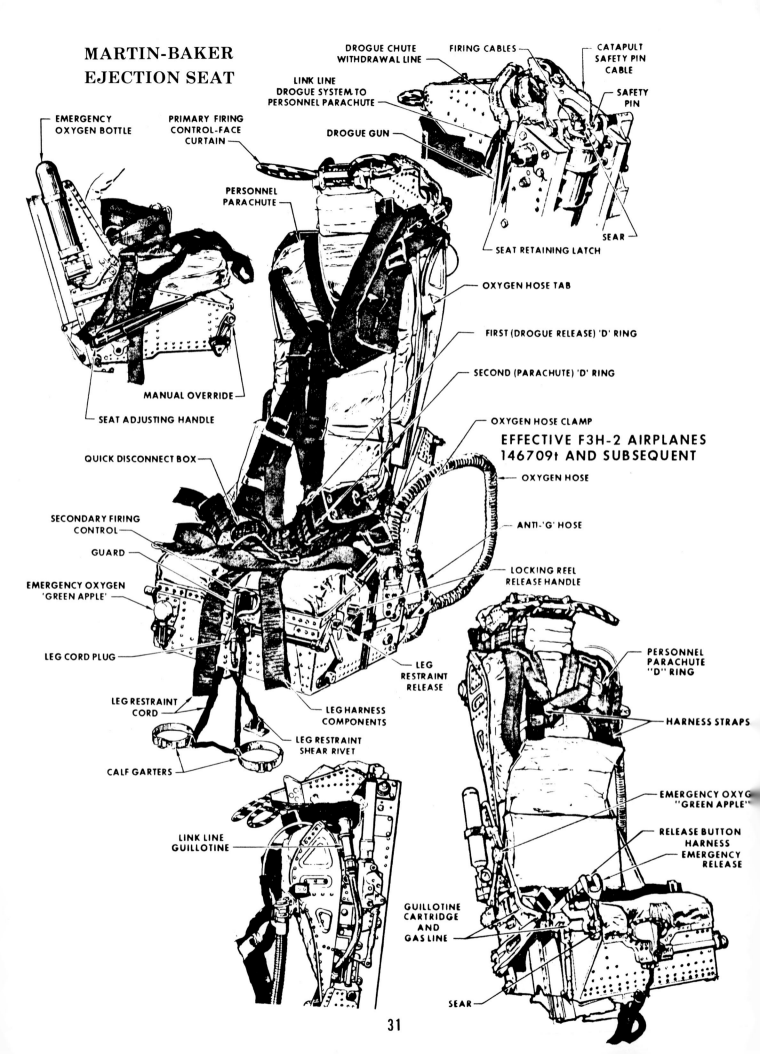

F3H-1N INSTRUMENT PANEL

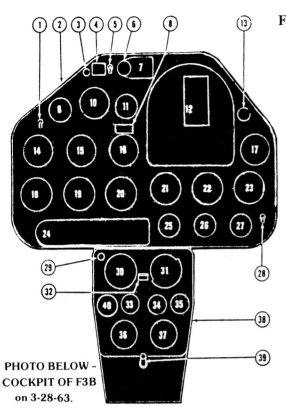

1. COMPASS CONTROL SWITCH
2. MAIN INSTRUMENT PANEL
3. PANEL ILLUMINATION LAMP (32)
4. LANDING CHECK LIST
5. FIRE TEST, WARNING LIGHTS TEST SWITCH
6. FIRE WARNING LIGHT
7. TAKE-OFF CHECK LIST
8. RADIO IDENTIFICATION NUMBER
9. ANGLE-OF-ATTACK INDICATOR
10. RADAR ALTIMETER
11. CLOCK
12. RADAR RANGE INDICATOR
13. CHECK HYDRAULIC GAUGES
14. AIR-SPEED INDICATOR & MACH METER
15. RADIO MAGNETIC INDICATOR
16. GYRO HORIZON INDICATOR
17. FUEL FLOW INDICATOR
18. ALTIMETER
19. RATE-OF-CLIMB INDICATOR
20. TURN-AND-BANK INDICATOR
21. ACCELEROMETER
22. SPACE FOR ID249 COURSE INDICATOR
23. FUEL QUANTITY INDICATOR
24. ARMAMENT CONTROL PANEL
25. TACHOMETER
26. TURBINE OUTLET TEMPERATURE
27. CABIN PRESSURE ALTIMETER
28. FUEL QUANTITY SELECT SWITCH
29. PANEL ILLUMINATION LAMP (11)
30. MASTER DIRECTION INDICATOR
31. ROCKET STATION SELECTOR SWITCH
32. OXYGEN HOSE CLIP
33. OIL PRESSURE INDICATOR
34. AFTERBURNER FUEL PRESSURE INDICATOR
35. FUEL BOOST PRESSURE INDICATOR
36. PNEUMATIC PRESSURE INDICATOR
37. POWER & UTILITY HYDRAULIC PRESSURE
38. PEDESTAL PANEL
39. RUDDER PEDAL ADJUSTMENT HANDLE
40. FUEL LOW WARNING LIGHT

PHOTO BELOW - COCKPIT OF F3B on 3-28-63.

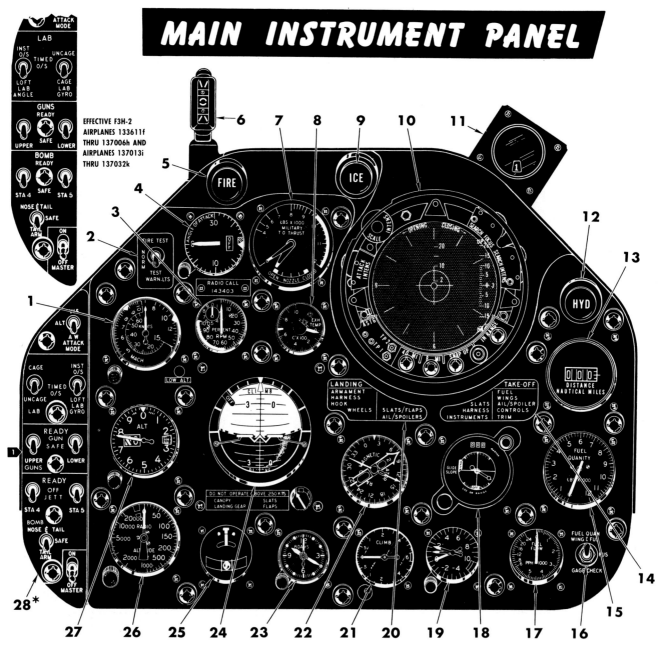

MAIN INSTRUMENT PANEL

EFFECTIVE F3H-2 AIRPLANES 133611f THRU 137006h AND AIRPLANES 137013i THRU 137032k

1. AIRSPEED AND MACHMETER
2. WARNING LIGHT & FIRE WARNING TEST SWITCH
3. TACHOMETER
4. ANGLE-OF-ATTACK INDICATOR
5. FIRE WARNING LIGHT
6. ANGLE-OF-ATTACK INDEXER
7. THRUST AND NOZZLE POSITION INDICATOR
8. EXHAUST TEMP. (E.G.T.) INDICATOR
9. ICE WARNING LIGHT (UPON THE INCORPORATION OF ASC188)
10. AN/APG-51C RADAR SCOPE
11. UHF REMOTE CHANNEL INDICATOR
12. HYD. PRESSURE WARNING LIGHT
13. TACAN RANGE INDICATOR
14. TAKE-OFF CHECK LIST
15. FUEL QUANTITY INDICATOR
16. FUEL QUANTITY GAGE CHECK SWITCH
17. FUEL FLOW INDICATOR
18. TACAN COURSE INDICATOR
19. ACCELEROMETER
20. LANDING CHECK LIST
21. RATE-OF-CLIMB INDICATOR
22. RADIO MAGNETIC INDICATOR
23. CLOCK
24. ATTITUDE GYRO
25. TURN AND SLIP INDICATOR
26. RADIO ALTIMETER
27. BAROMETRIC ALTIMETER
28. ARMAMENT CONTROL PANEL

*EFFECTIVE F3H-2 AIRPLANES 137006h THRU 137012h, 143403m AND UP

EFFECTIVE F3H-2m AIRPLANES 133549d THRU 133610f

1 UPON THE INCORPORATION OF ASC 169 THE UPPER GUN SWITCH IS REMOVED

RIGHT CONSOLE

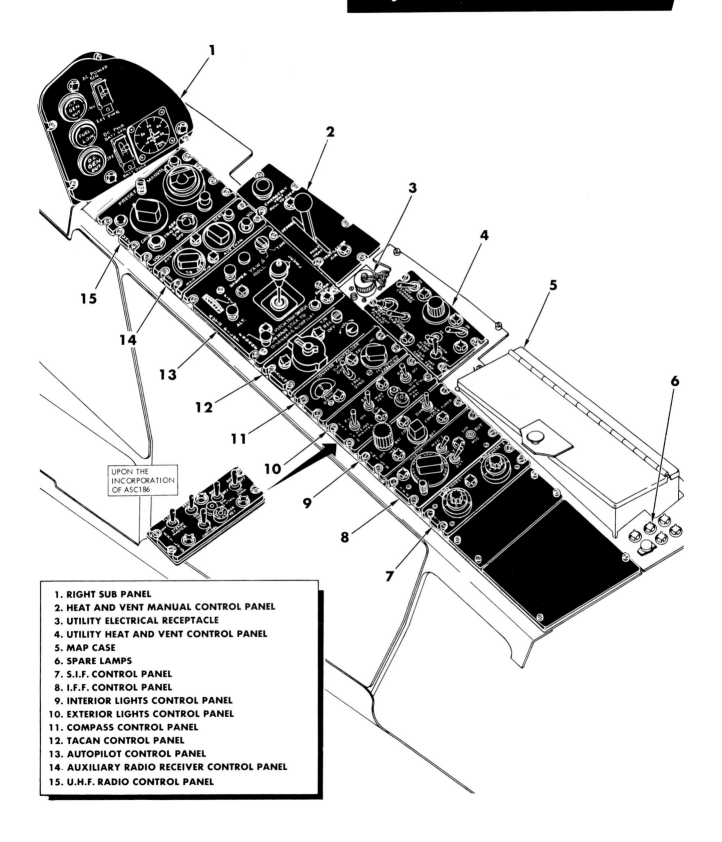

1. RIGHT SUB PANEL
2. HEAT AND VENT MANUAL CONTROL PANEL
3. UTILITY ELECTRICAL RECEPTACLE
4. UTILITY HEAT AND VENT CONTROL PANEL
5. MAP CASE
6. SPARE LAMPS
7. S.I.F. CONTROL PANEL
8. I.F.F. CONTROL PANEL
9. INTERIOR LIGHTS CONTROL PANEL
10. EXTERIOR LIGHTS CONTROL PANEL
11. COMPASS CONTROL PANEL
12. TACAN CONTROL PANEL
13. AUTOPILOT CONTROL PANEL
14. AUXILIARY RADIO RECEIVER CONTROL PANEL
15. U.H.F. RADIO CONTROL PANEL

LEFT CONSOLE

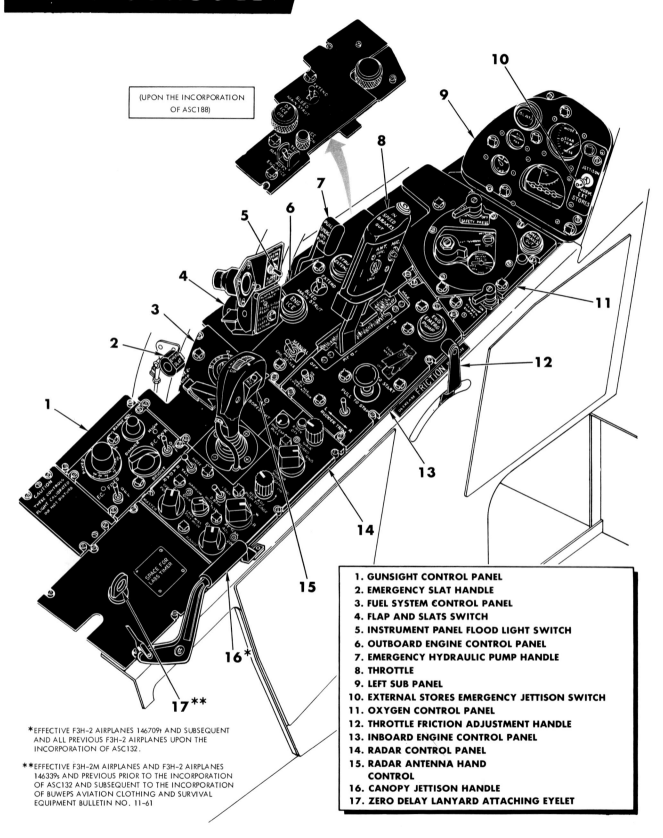

(UPON THE INCORPORATION OF ASC188)

1. GUNSIGHT CONTROL PANEL
2. EMERGENCY SLAT HANDLE
3. FUEL SYSTEM CONTROL PANEL
4. FLAP AND SLATS SWITCH
5. INSTRUMENT PANEL FLOOD LIGHT SWITCH
6. OUTBOARD ENGINE CONTROL PANEL
7. EMERGENCY HYDRAULIC PUMP HANDLE
8. THROTTLE
9. LEFT SUB PANEL
10. EXTERNAL STORES EMERGENCY JETTISON SWITCH
11. OXYGEN CONTROL PANEL
12. THROTTLE FRICTION ADJUSTMENT HANDLE
13. INBOARD ENGINE CONTROL PANEL
14. RADAR CONTROL PANEL
15. RADAR ANTENNA HAND CONTROL
16. CANOPY JETTISON HANDLE
17. ZERO DELAY LANYARD ATTACHING EYELET

*EFFECTIVE F3H-2 AIRPLANES 146709† AND SUBSEQUENT AND ALL PREVIOUS F3H-2 AIRPLANES UPON THE INCORPORATION OF ASC132.

**EFFECTIVE F3H-2M AIRPLANES AND F3H-2 AIRPLANES 146339s AND PREVIOUS PRIOR TO THE INCORPORATION OF ASC132 AND SUBSEQUENT TO THE INCORPORATION OF BUWEPS AVIATION CLOTHING AND SURVIVAL EQUIPMENT BULLETIN NO. 11-61

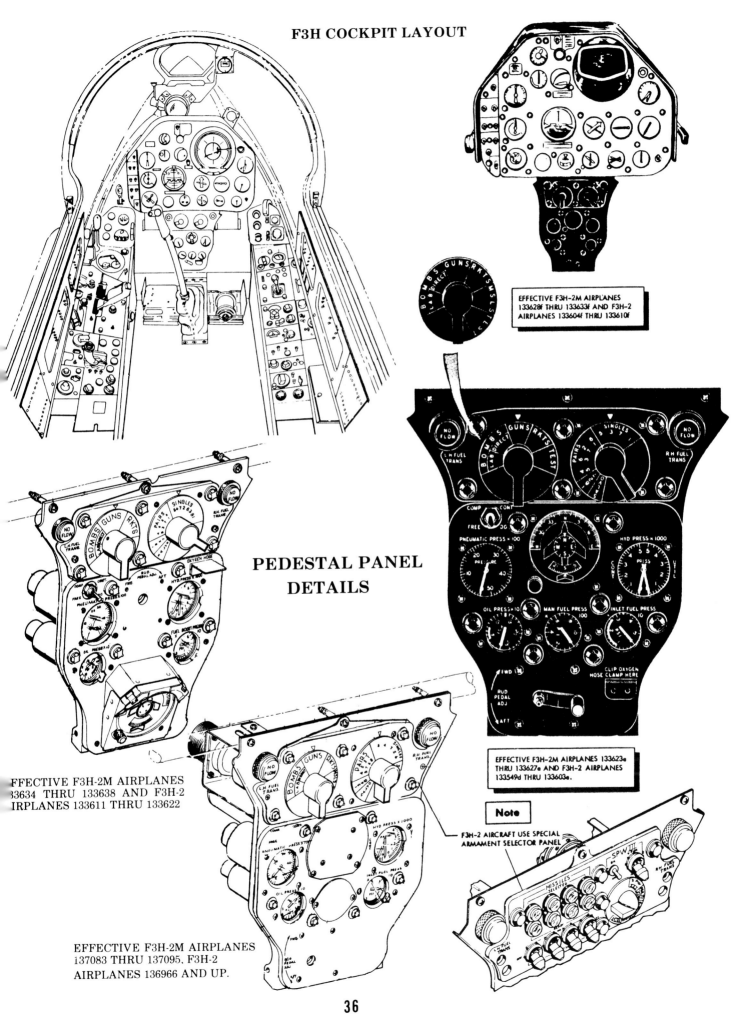

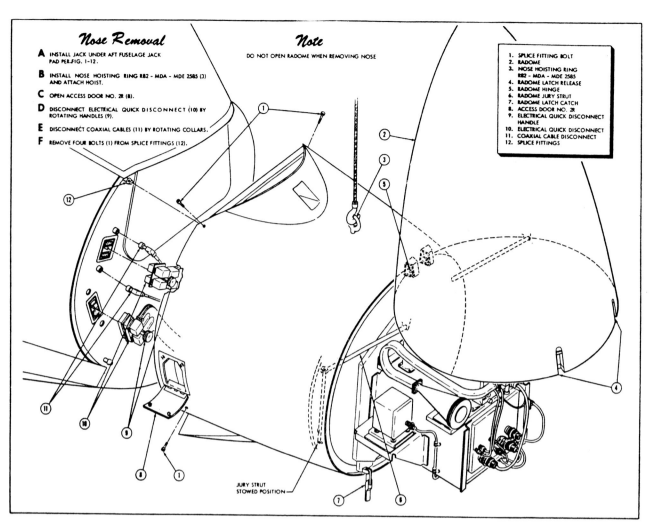

F3H-1N RADAR

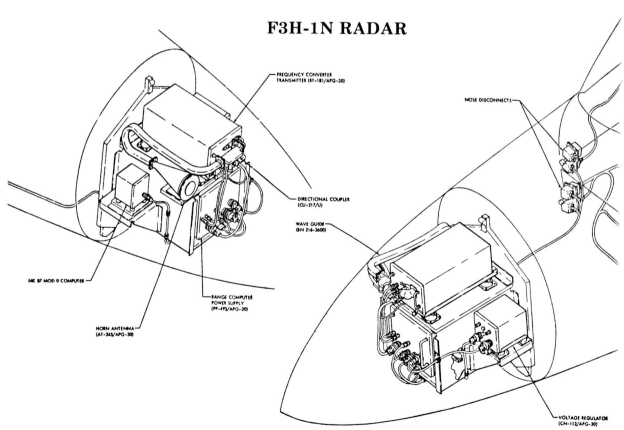

F3H-2 RADAR

INDEX NO.	NOMENCLATURE
1	Antenna - AN/APG-51B Radar
2	Receiver-Transmitter - AN/APG-51B
3	Antenna - AT-234/APX IFF
4	Pump - AN/APA-127 Gear
5	Tank - AN/APA-127 Expansion
6	Exchanger - AN/APA-127 Heat
7	Piping - Magnetron Cooling
8	Plug - Nose Radar
9	Indicator - RT-178/ARC-27A Remote Channel
10	Indicator - Flight
11	Indicator - Radar Altimeter
12	Indicator - Course
13	Gun Sight - MK 11 Mod 1 or MK 11 Mod 3
14	Control - AN/ARC-27A UHF Radio Set
15	Control - AN/ARR-40
16	Control - AN/APX-6 IFF
17	Resistor - Radio Compass
18	Unit - AN/ARN-21 Radio Compass
19	Panel - Circuit Breaker
20	Shelf - Computer Compartment Equipment
21	Computer - MK 86 Mod 0
22	Antenna - Lower UHF
23	Switch - UHF Radio Coaxial
24	Relay - Antenna Solenoid
25	Receiver-Transmitter - AN/ARC-27 UHF Radio
26	Relay - Radio Magnetic Indicator Slaving
27	Antenna - AT-234/APX IFF
28	Amplifier - Damper Control
29	Amplifier - AN/APN-22 Electronic Control
30	Amplifier - AN/ARA-25 Electrical Control
31	Rack - AN/APA-127 Mounting
32	Power Supply - AN/APA-127
33	Panel - Fuse & Circuit Breaker Left Side
34	Adapter - Antenna IFF
35	Switch - Throttle Grip Microphone
36	Horn - Pseudo Signal
37	Control - AN/APG-51B Radar Set
38	Panel Assembly - Gun Sight Control
39	Disconnect Assembly - Pilot Composite
40	Mount - AN/APX-6 IFF Receiver -Transmitter
41	Panel - Fuse & Circuit Breaker Right Side
42	Plug - AN/ARC-27 Coaxial
43	Cable - Coaxial
44	Jack - Coaxial
45	Mount - AN/ARA-25 Electrical Control Amplifier
46	Mount - Receiver/Transmitter UHF Radio
47	Antenna - AN/ARA-25 Radio
48	Plug & Cable - Coaxial
49	Antenna - AN/ARN-21 Navigational Radio
50	Transmitter - Compass
51	Receiver-Transmitter - AN/APN-22 Radar Altimeter
52	Housing - AN/APN-22 Receiver -Transmitter
53	Receiver - AN/ARR-40 Radio

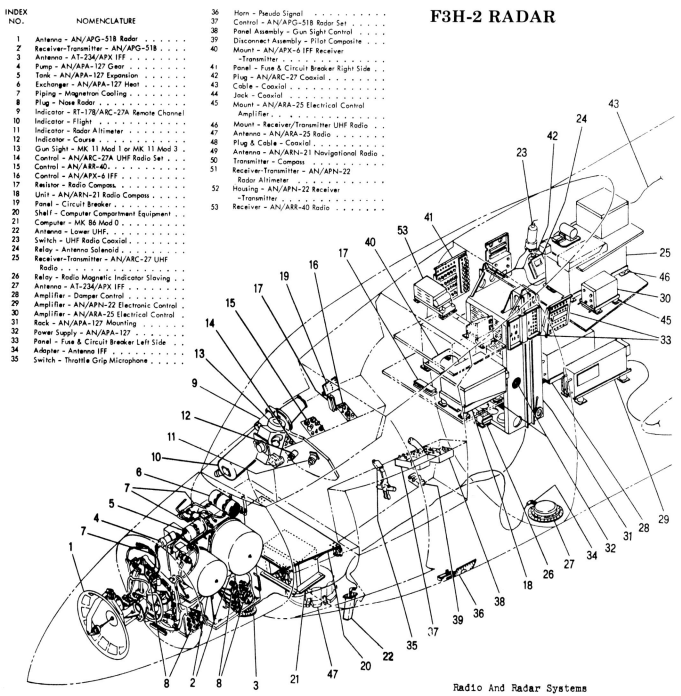

Radio And Radar Systems

Removable Nose

F3H-2

1. PUMP, AN/APA-127 GEAR
2. TANK, AN/APA-127 EXPANSION
3. VALVE, THREE-WAY
4. BOLT
5. EXCHANGER, AN/APA-127 HEAT
6. TWIST ASSEMBLY, AN/APA-127 45°
7. COUPLER, AN/APA-127 DIRECTIONAL
8. ISOLATOR ASSEMBLY, AN/APA-127
9. COVER, FILTER
10. SCREW
11. FILTER ASSEMBLY, AN/APA-127
12. MAGNETRON ASSEMBLY AN/APA-127
13. AMPLIFIER, SYNCHRO
14. POWER SUPPLY, LOW VOLTAGE
15. AMPLIFIER ASSEMBLY
16. CONVERTER, SIGNAL DATA
17. BOX INTERCONNECTING
18. AMPLIFIER, ELECTRONIC CONTROL
19. SYNCHRONIZER
20. RECEIVER-TRANSMITTER
21. BOLT
22. SWITCH & RADIO FREQUENCY DUMMY LOAD ASSEMBLY
23. ANTENNA
24. ROD FERRITE ANTENNA
25. MOUNT, ANTENNA
26. BOLT
27. TRANSDUCER, AIR STREAM DIRECTOR
28. ELBOW
29. TRANSDUCER, ANGEL OF ATTACK
30. SCREW
31. PLATE ASSEMBLY
32. RING
33. TRANSMITTER
34. ANTENNA, STABILIZATION UNIT
35. CAP

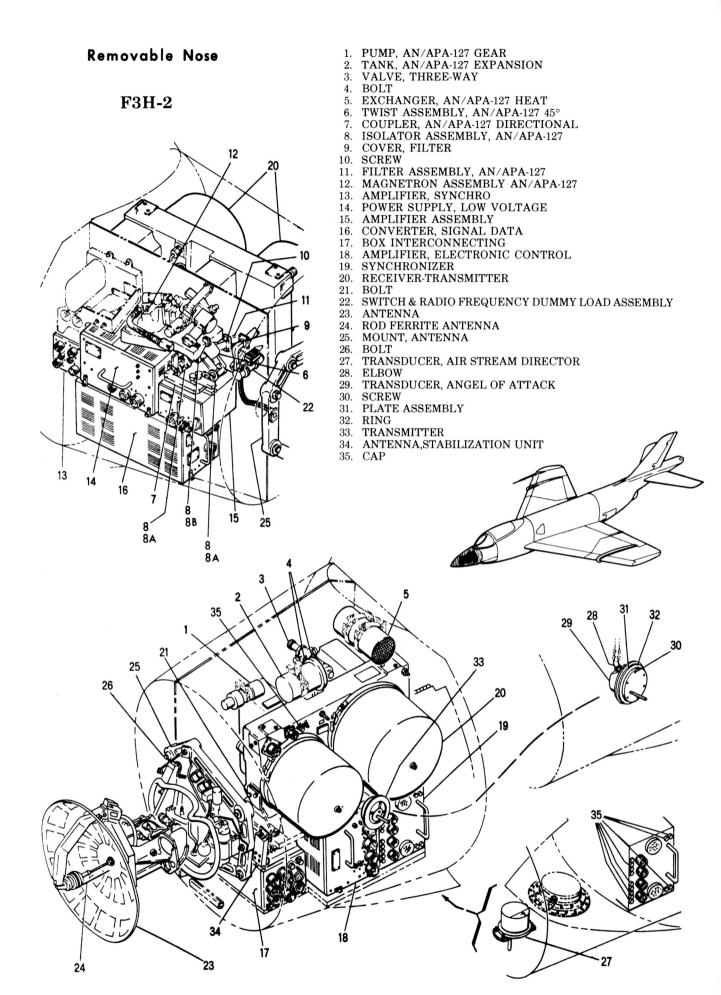

Nose Radar Instruments Installation (AN/APG-51B)

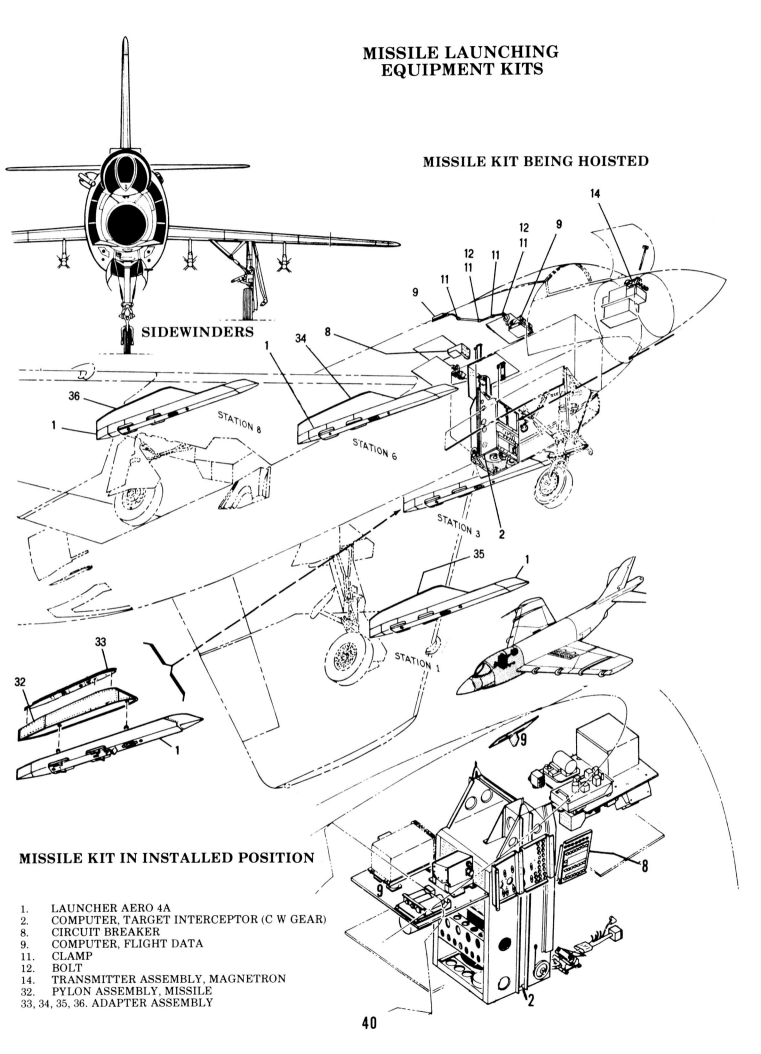

MISSILE LAUNCHING EQUIPMENT KITS

MISSILE KIT BEING HOISTED

SIDEWINDERS

MISSILE KIT IN INSTALLED POSITION

1. LAUNCHER AERO 4A
2. COMPUTER, TARGET INTERCEPTOR (C W GEAR)
8. CIRCUIT BREAKER
9. COMPUTER, FLIGHT DATA
11. CLAMP
12. BOLT
14. TRANSMITTER ASSEMBLY, MAGNETRON
32. PYLON ASSEMBLY, MISSILE
33, 34, 35, 36. ADAPTER ASSEMBLY

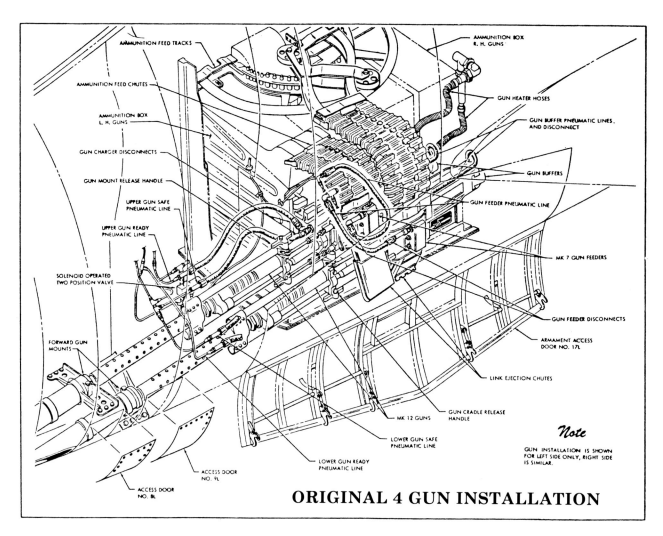

ORIGINAL 4 GUN INSTALLATION

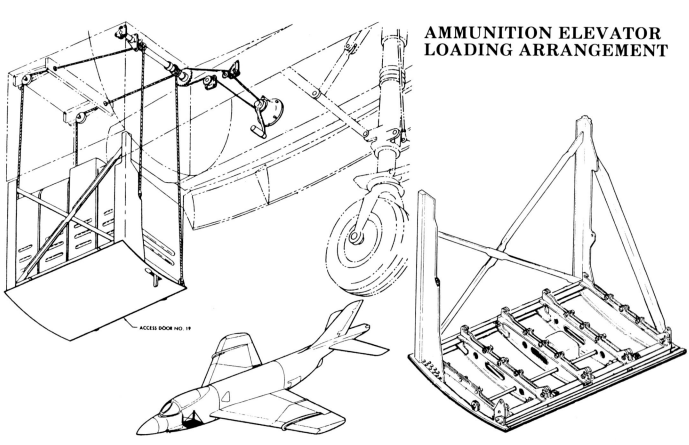

AMMUNITION ELEVATOR LOADING ARRANGEMENT

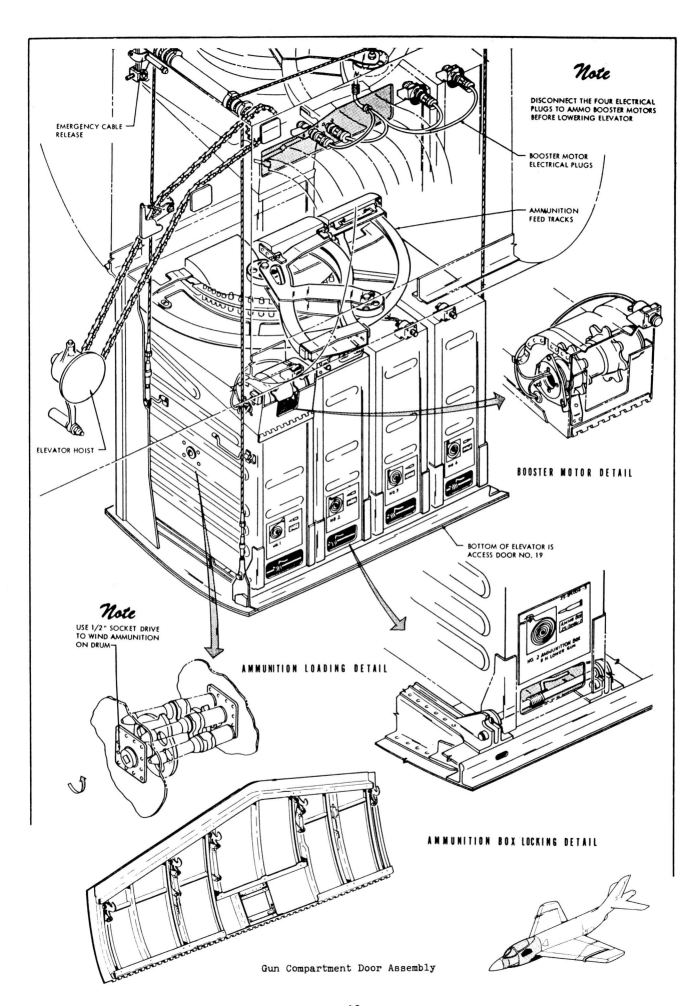

PHOTO ABOVE — Publicity photo of F3H-2N, 137020, with its adoptted Allison J71 engine which replaced the ill fatted Westinghouse J40.

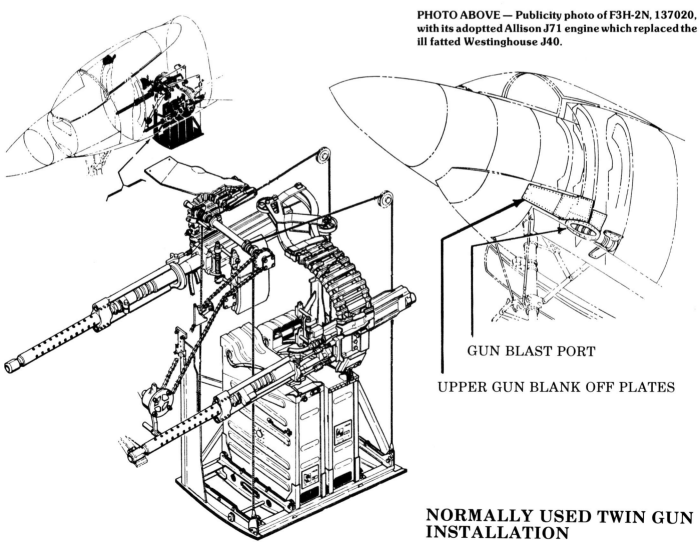

GUN BLAST PORT

UPPER GUN BLANK OFF PLATES

NORMALLY USED TWIN GUN INSTALLATION

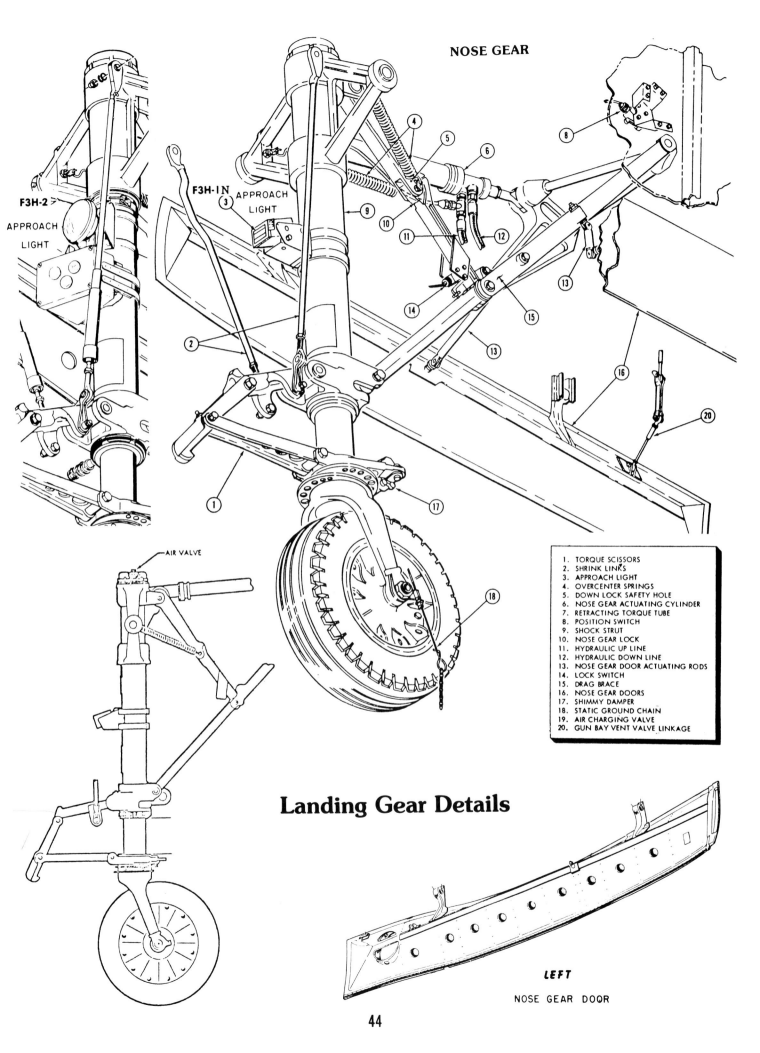

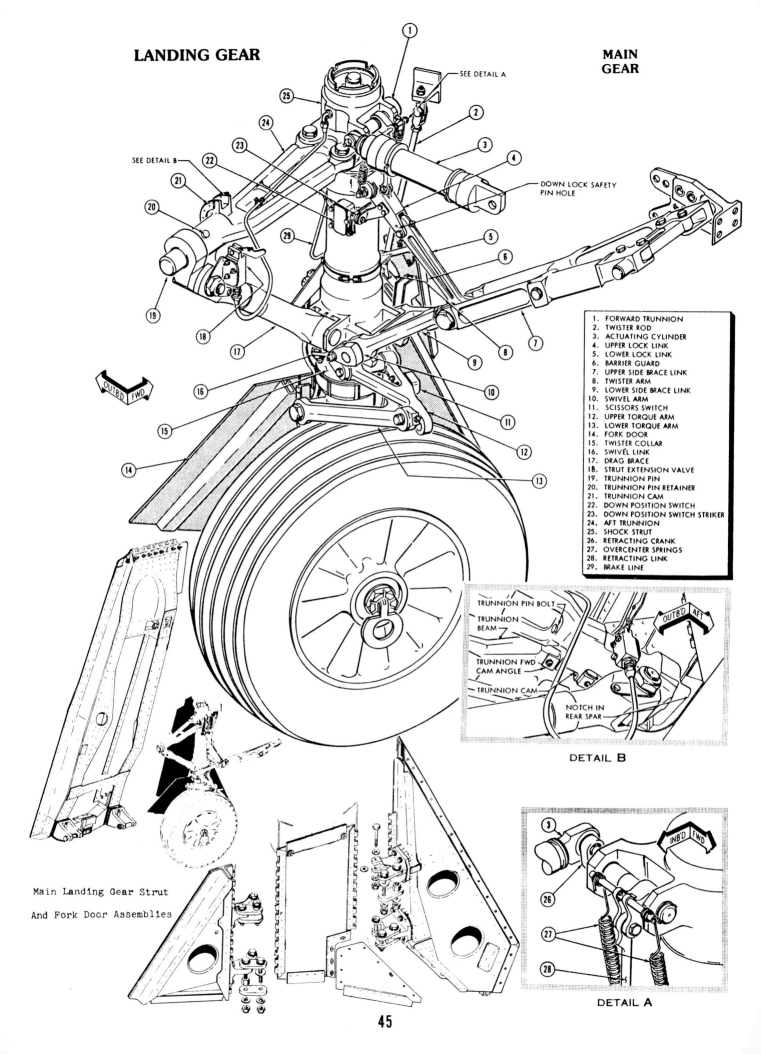

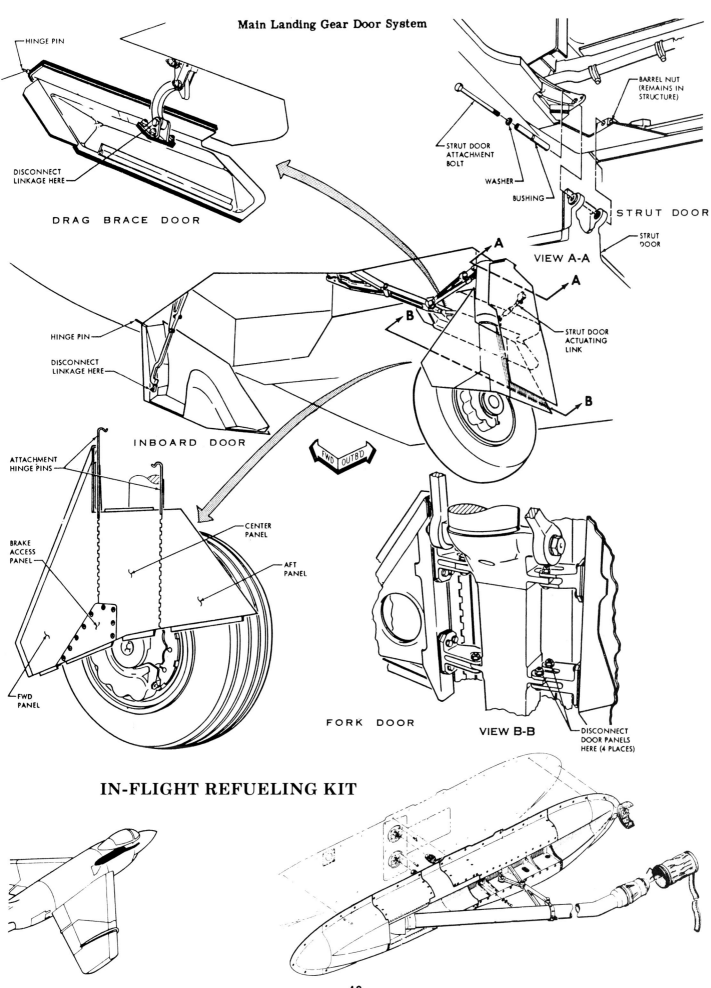

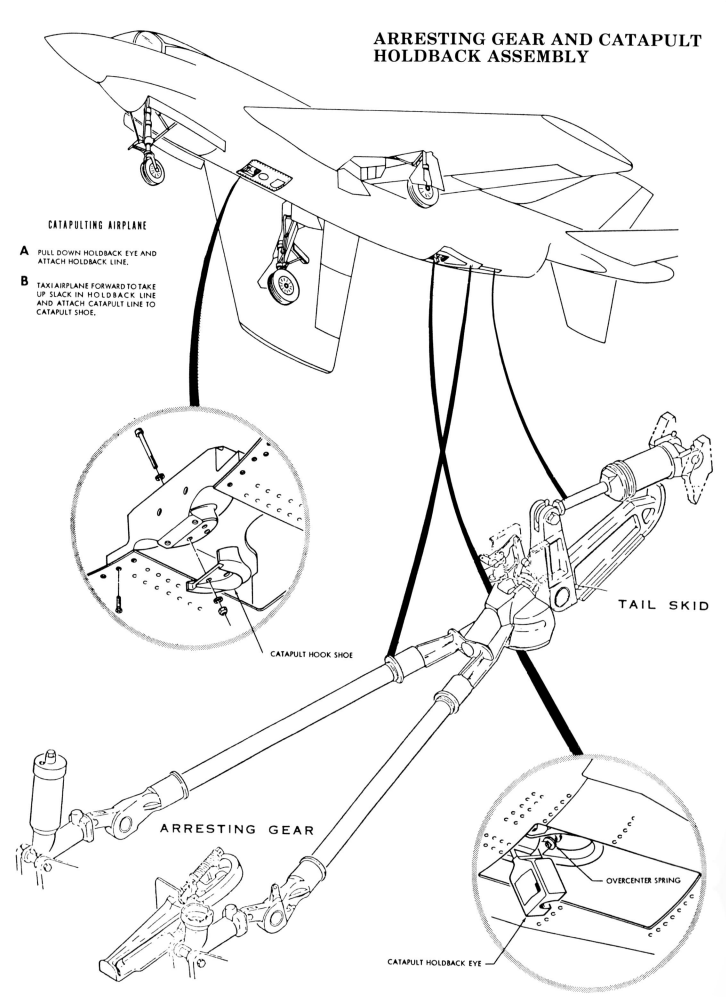

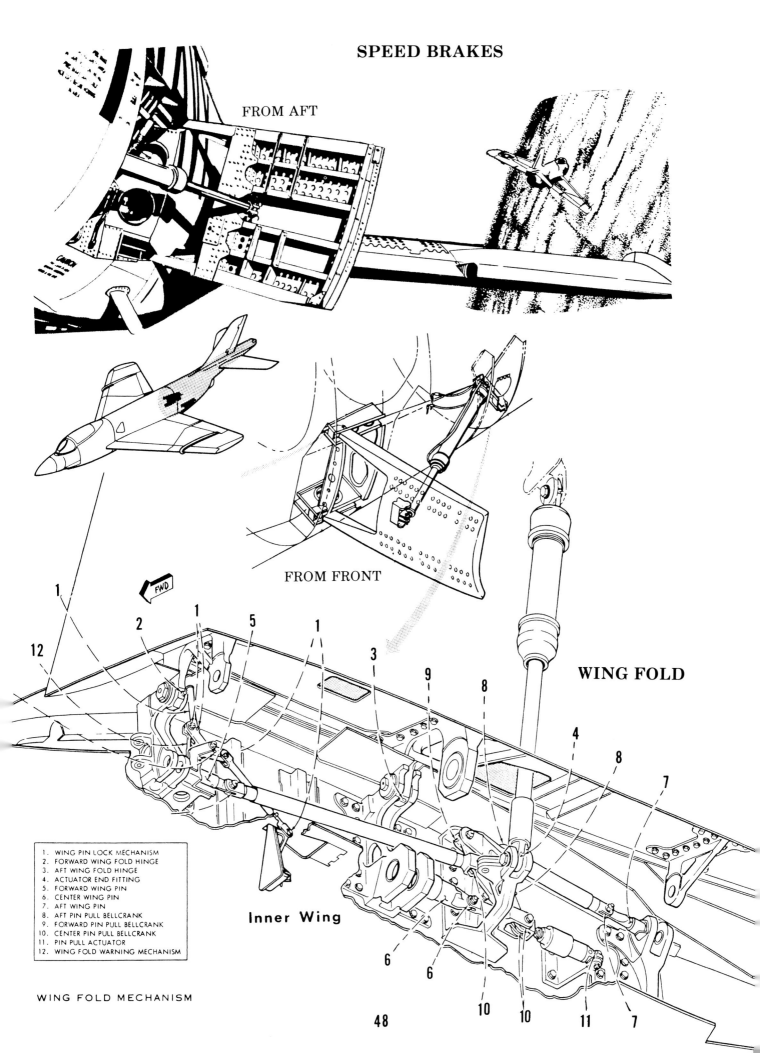

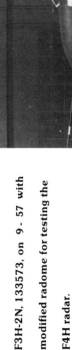

F3H-2N, 133573, on 9-57 with modified radome for testing the F4H radar.

F3H-2 INTERIOR ARRANGEMENT

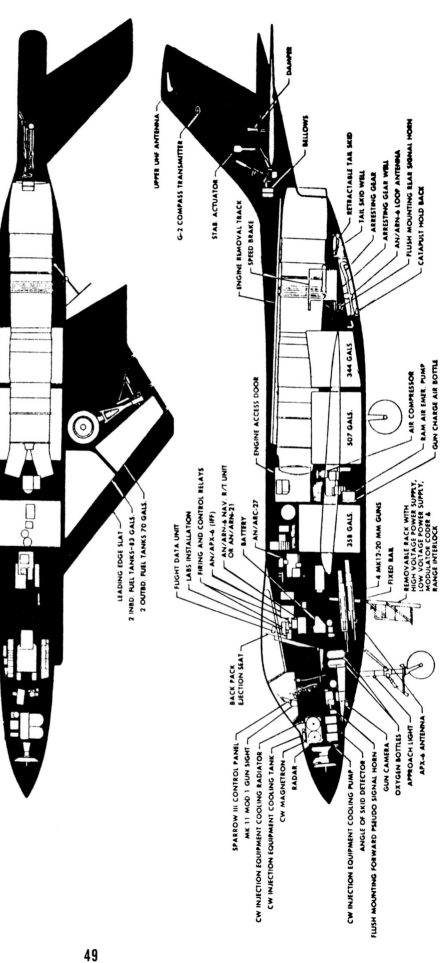

PLASTIC DEMON
Rareplanes 1/72 Scale F3H Demon by Tommy Thomason

The Rareplanes F3H-2 Demon is a 1/72 scale vacuform of this big fighter. The kit includes cast metal landing gear and a refueling probe. As usual, surface detail is accomplished with a combination of raised and engraved lines. Gordon Stevens has paid a lot of attention to other details as well. The vacuform parts include the inlet interior, internal canopy structure, and a Martin-Baker ejection seat. Assembly has been facilitated with features like an integral tab on the fuselage for the vertical fin and bulkheads that fit.

The kit comes with two external tanks and four missile pylons. One F3H story is that only one tank was used because the aircraft couldn't fly as far on two tanks as it could with one due to interference drag between the tanks. As late as 1962, however, the Pilot's Manual stated that two tanks could be carried.

The outline was checked against a set of 1/72 scale line drawings provided by Greg Kuklinski. The basic outline is excellent except for the canopy, which fails to completely capture the big bulged shape of the windshield side panels. In addition, the underside of the beavertail was concave back to the horizontal tail.

The main landing gear lacks the drag link which extends aft from the main strut into the other slot in the wing. (There should also be a gear door on the inboard side of this slot.)

The nose gear has some shortcomings. The antitorque link should be three sided as shown in the drawing. The nose wheel hub is proportionally a little large, with small holes which shouldn't be there. The nose gear butts to the bottom of the fuselage instead of extending into a realistic wheel well. Incidentally, a small tail skid extended when the gear was down; this is not shown on the kit drawing.

The cockpit components provided are a tub, instrument panel, and ejection seat. The seat is vacuformed but detailed enough to recognize as a Martin-Baker type which was installed in latter Demons and retrofitted to some. I cut down the sides of the tub in order to add consoles. A realistic cockpit is a little difficult to obtain because of the inlet interior which essentially doubles the fuselage wall thickness in the cockpit area.

Installation of the inlet interior takes a lot of trimming and fitting. I recommend that you cut out the intake only at first, so that the top of the cockpit holds the forward fuselage in position while you're trying to get the inlet interior to fit. Once its glued in place, you can go ahead and open up the top of the fuselage.

The first production aircraft delivered (to VF-14 in March 1956?) did not have spoilers, the pitot on the right wing tip, Martin-Baker seats, or the refueling probe. (Preproduction aircraft by the way, had a one piece windscreen, different gunsight, and a pitot on the underside of the fuselage ahead of the nose gear.) The spoilers are the perforated panels on the upper surface of the inboard wing; they were not originally on -2Ns, BuNos 133549 through 133610, or -2M's 133569 or 133623 through 137040. The Martin-Baker seats were installed in BuNos 146709 through 146740 at the factory. The only other significant production change is that the beavertail was reduced in length on BuNos 143403 and subsequent. Finally, the two upper 20mm cannons were removed from the aircraft at some point during their service life.

This is a better than average vacuform kit of an aircraft which illustrates the transition in the Navy from the subsonic straight wing F2H Banshee to the Mach 2 Phantom. The presence of cast metal landing gear in this kit also reduces the modeling effort and skill required.

Ginter built model of Rareplane Demon in one of the many different VF-31 schemes. Tail stripes and wing-tips are red.

Two more views of the Rareplanes Demon. Note that canopy does not capture the big bulged shape of the side panels. A bent straight pin was used to reproduce the right wing pitot-tube. Very often Demon Sidewinders were dark blue with white noses as shown on the model.

BELOW — Is an illustration drawing from the 1970s Airmodel vacuform kit of the Demon. The kit was as crude as the drawing and is not recommended.

While attached to the Naval Air Test Center, Patuxent River, Maryland, George Watkins and Cal Callaway had the following reactions to the Demon.

Cal Callaway and Mine Testing.

The F3H we had at Armament Test division was reputed to be the prototype F3H-2N, meaning it was a F3H-1 with the airframe modified to accept the 2N engine. I have no reason to doubt the story as the aircraft was still painted blue and was one of the last jets so painted except for the F9F-8. Also an F3H twenty BuNos earlier than the one we were flying was set in concrete on display at the Naval Academy.

At the time, we were doing a series of mine tests at ArmTest getting flight time on various mines. We hung them on whatever we had and logged time on them at various airspeeds to test the structural integrity or wheather arming wires pulled out, etc. We started at slow speeds and worked up in increments with the last series of tests being 15 min. at 600 KIAS. The only thing we had that could haul a 2,000 lb. mine at that speed was the Demon. We would take off, climb to about 10,000 feet, push over in afterburner, come down over the bay at 600K and about 500 feet, run until we were low on fuel, pull up and head for the field. We ususally got about 5 min. on a 600K hop.

As you might imagine, these hops were not eagerly sought after in the office. I confessed one day that I didn't really relish those hops and that I did, in fact lower the seat all the way down as I descended and just peeked over the edge of the cockpit while getting the 600K time. I did this because I was terrified by the sea gulls going by. Turned out everyone in the shop was just as scared and did the same thing. Luckily we never hit one — guess they were pushed aside by the 'Brute' at that speed.

George Watkings and the F3H

I first started flying the F3H at Patuxent River, NATC, in 1955. I was responsible for performing the following tests; stability and control, handling qualities, fuel consumption and performance.

We had moved up to NAS Atlantic City in the middle of 1956 to carry on some high priority flying projects while the main runway at Patuxent River was undergoing emergency repairs. My project was to check the flying qualities and performance characteristics of the Demon with six 500 lb. bombs attached. From our tests we determined that this airplane was probably the shortest legged fighter that was ever built by man, when used in the attack role. It also turned out to be a very poor delivery platform.

On one of my first flights in this attack configuration, I developed a serious hydraulic leak. This eventually caused a complete lack of brake pressure on the right wheel — as determined while still airborne. In those days, this was considered one of the more serious emergencies, because there was no cable arresting gear across the runways (later installed at all Naval Air Stations) to arrest the airplane by its tailhook. As the loss of hydraulic fluid and pressure occurred late in the flight, I had relatively little fuel left. First I had to get rid of those six 500 lb. general purpose bombs! I didn't even know, at that moment, whether these bombs were inert or regular bombs without any arming mechanisms installed. But no matter, the bombs wouldn't release anyway — they

PHOTO BELOW — NATC YF3H-2, 133631, assigned to Systems Test Division, in 1958. Aircraft is gull-grey and white, note inside of gear doors are red. Also note auxillary fuel-tank pylon silver landing gear with white wheels.

had not been hooked up electrically and the manual release handle, when pulled, did nothing! I was now down to just 300 lbs. of internal fuel, which for a Demon with 3,000 lbs. of external stores, is good for about two minutes of flying time. I decided to land on the non-duty runway with the crosswind coming from the side with the failed braking system. Fortunately it worked and I was able to stop the airplane at the far end of the runway. I didn't even have to shut down the engine as I had flamed out on touch down.

PHOTO ABOVE — F3H-2M, 133627, assigned to NATC Armament Testing Division, equipped with dark blue Sparrow I missiles, in flight over its home base a NAS Paxtuxent River. USN photo via Clay Jannson. PHOTO BELOW — F3H-2, 137009, at a open house in 1958. Note the AT21 under cockpit which stands for Armament Test. Note Sparrow III missiles and extended refueling boom. R.F. Besecker photo.

BESIDES NATC ARMAMENT TEST, MANY OTHER NAVAL FACILITIES TESTED DEMON WEAPON SYSTEMS. THEY WERE NAVAL AIR ORDANANCE TEST CENTER (NAOTS) CHINCUEAGE, NAVAL ORDANANCE TEST CENTER (NOTS) (NWC) CHINA LAKE, NAVAL WEAPONS EVALUATION FACILITY (NWEF), NAVAL MISSILE CENTER (NMC) POINT MUGU AND VX-4.

PHOTO ABOVE — Poor USN photo of early F3H-2N assigned to NAOTS Chincueage in 1955. Blue overall with white outer wing panels and fin tip. Note 2,000 lb. bomb on fuselage pylon and rocket pak on the outer wing pylon.

Naval Air Facility, China Lake

The U.S. Naval Air Facility, China Lake, California, provided support to the U.S. Naval Ordnance Test Station (NOTS), China Lake, for research, development, test and evaluation of guided missles, aircraft weapons delivery systems, aircraft rockets and rocket launchers, aviation fire control systems, and underwater ordnance.

PHOTO AT RIGHT — 1984 Naval Weapons Center insignia. Colors are black boarder with white lettering and missiles, golden brown Eagle and anchor, red lightning bolts and a blue background. Ginter photo.

PHOTO BELOW — Direct from the factory and still carrying its McDonnell #81 construction number on its tail, F3H-2N, 133569, sits on the ramp at NAS China Lake. The aircraft is fitted with a test boom and six conventional weapons pylons, so that the Demon can be evaluated in the ground attack role. Colors are gull grey and white with red day-glo nose, gear doors, wing tips, inboard horizontal tail surfaces and two vertical tail stripes. USN photo on 22 May 1956.

PHOTOS ABOVE — F3H-2, 133550, on take off and in the air with a Douglas F3D Skyknight (see Naval Fighters #4). Note this is the first photo I have seen of a Skyknight carrying a Sidewinder. USN photos circa 1958.

PHOTO BELOW — F3H-2, 133565, at a NAS China Lake open house in 1958. Standard gull-grey and white scheme, note that usually the rudder is gull-grey on Demons, also note that the nose is from a different Demon. D. Olson photo via W.T. Larkins.

PHOTOS: TOP — F3H-2, 136990, from NWEF (NAVAL WEAPONS EVALUATION FACILITY) at Litchfield Park on 18 March 1963. D. Olson via C. Jannson. Aircraft is overall white with day-glo nose, tail and forward half of the wings.
MIDDLE — F3H-2N, 133555, from NASWF (NAVAL AVIATION SPECIAL WEAPONS FACILITY) which is the same organization as NWEF. Day-glo orange tail and wing tip. Via D. Spering.

The Naval Air Test Facility (Ship Installations), NAS Lakehurst, New Jersey, had the mission of research, development, testing and evaluation of shipboard and shore based catapult and arresting systems.

BOTTOM TWO PHOTOS — F3H-2N, 133575, from Naval Air Test Facility Lakehurst (NATF). Aircraft is gull-grey and white with day-glo nose and tail. Tail stripe is red boardered by white and then black. In taxi photo taken on 9-13-63 F3H has a white rudder, ground shot taken in 1960 has a grey rudder. Photos by R.F. Besecker.

DEMON SQUADRONS 1956 to 1964

CVG	1956 CODE	1956 SQD.	1957 CODE	1957 SQD.	1958 SQD.	1959 SQD.	1960 SQD.	1961 SQD.	1962 SQD.	1963 SQD.	1964 SDQ.
AIRLANT SQUADRONS											
CVG-1	T	VF-14	AB	VF-14	VF-14	VF-14	VF-14	VF-14	VF-14	VF-14	
CVG-3	K	VF-31	AC	VF-31	VF-31	VF-31	VF-31	VF-31	VF-31	VF-31	
RCVG-4			AD		VF-101	VF-101	VF-101	VF-101			
ATG-181			AM		VF-41						
CVG-7	L	*VF-61	AG	*VF-61	*VF-61	VF-41	VF-41	VF-41	VF-41		
CVG-8	E	*VF-61	AJ	*VF-61	*VF-61						
CVG-8	E	VF-82	AJ	VF-82	VF-82						
CVG-10			AK						VF-13	VF-13	VF-13
CVG-13			AE					VF-131	VF-131		
CVG-16			AH				VF-161	VF-161			
AIRPAC SQUADRONS											
CVG-2			NE	VF-24	VF-24	VF-21	VF-21	VF-21	VF-21		
CVG-2			NE		VF-64	VF-64					
CVG-5			NF		VF-53	VF-53	VF-53	VF-53	VF-54	VF-54	
CVG-5			NF						VF-92		
CVG-9			NG	VF-122	VF-122	VF-92	VF-92	VF-92			
CVG-11	V	VF-112	NH	VF-112	VF-112	VF-112					
ATG-1			NA		VF-112	VF-112					
CVG-11			NH	VF-114	VF-114	VF-114	VF-114				
RCVG-12	D	VF-124	NJ	VF-124	VF-121	VF-121	VF-121	VF-121			
CVG-14			NK		VF-141	VF-141	VF-141	VF-141			
CVG-15			NL		VF-151	VF-151	VF-151	VF-151	VF-151		
CVG-16			AH						VF-161	VF-161	VF-161
CVG-19			NM	VF-193	VF-193	VF-193	VF-193	VF-193	VF-193		
CVG-21			NP	VF-24	VF-213	VF-213	VF-213	VF-213	VF-213	VF-213	

NOTE - SQUADRONS ARE MARKED IN YEAR EVEN IF THEY HAD DEMONS FOR ONLY ONE MONTH

* ALTHOUGH ASSIGNED TO CVG-6, VF-61 ONLY CARRIED CVG-7 and 8 TAIL CODES

OTHER SQUADRONS   VC-3/VF(AW)-3 TAILCODE NP, VX-3 TAILCODE XC, VX-4 TAILCODE XF.

VX-4 patch, boarder, lettering and ocean medium blue. Sky and background for lettering gold. Missile and continents grey. Red neutron tracks, missile flame and sun and hash marks on a white field. White stars. Photo by Steve Ginsberg.

AT RIGHT — Recent PMTC emblem, lettering and background dark blue with golden-brown Eagle and anchor. BELOW — Two views of F3H-2, 146736, taken in the early sixties by W. Swisher. Top view shows 736 in standard gull-grey and white scheme. Bottom view shows 736 in overall white with day-glo tail, nose and forward half of wing. Note beaver tail and engine are removed.

PHOTOS: TOP — F3B, 133566, on 10-21-62 by W. Swisher. Note non-standard white rudder and red and white candystripped wing pitot-tube and trailing edge fuel dump. MIDDLE — F3B, 143468, in 1966 via C. Jannson. Grey and white scheme with day-glo nose, upper tail and outer wings, not black painted area behind aft fuselage oil vent. BOTTOM — F3H-2M, 133629, in grey and white scheme armed with Sparrow I missiles, note the natural metal plates used to blank off the gunports. Sept. 1956 photo by Bowers via Larkins.

PHOTOS: TOP — 5-19-62 photo of F3H-2, 133554, armed with white and blue Sparrow III missiles on the outer pylons and Sidewinders on the inner pylons. Photo by Swisher. MIDDLE — USN photo of F3H-2N, 137010, firing a Sparrow III missile. BOTTOM — F3H-2, 137011, on 12-2-59 firing a Sparrow III at a F9F drone during operation Top Gun. USN photo.

PHOTOS: TOP — Another shot of F3H-2, 137011. BOTTOM — Another function at Pt. Mugu is to provide targets. Here a JD-1 takes a KDA drone up to be used as a target for Sparrow III missiles during the Naval Air Weapons Meet on 30 Nov. 1959. USN photo.

PHOTOS: TOP — F3H-2M, 137051, on the taxi strip with a XKD4R-1 target drone on 2-11-58. USN via Wyckoff. MIDDLE — F3B, 133581, with a Beechcraft AQM-37A Supersonic Target missile. Beechcraft via Don Spering. BOTTOM — All white with day-glo tail F3B, 143484, with a Sparrow air two-stage, solid-propellant space probe on 9-13-63. USN via Wyckoff. The probe, one of five made, was launched in a nearly vertical attitude at 30,000 ft. and reached an alititude of 66 mi. The probe measured ultraviolet radiation from the stars.

VX-4

AIR DEVELOPMENT SQUADRON FOUR

Commissioned in 1950 on the East Coast, VX-4 was initially charged with the develoment of multi-engine Airborne Early Warning (AEW) radar planes and systems. From the New England area, VX-4 moved to NAS Patuxent River, Maryland in 1951. Shortly thereafter, with its AEW projects completed, VX-4 was decommissioned in order to form one complete AEW squadron as well as the nucleus for several others.

PHOTOS BELOW: TOP — Belly view of VX-4 Demon with four dayglo Sparrow I missiles. Nose gear doors are white and blue stripes. Note blue wing and horizontal stabjlizer tips. BOTTOM — F3H-2M, 137038, with blue Sparrow I missiles. Fin tip is blue with a red boarder and white stars. Note F6F red drones in background. USN photos via Wyckoff.

On 15 Sept. 1952, VX-4 was brought into being at its current home, Naval Missile Center, Point Mugu, Calif. The squadron was recommissioned under the command of CDR. James G. Sliney. The squadrons new misssion was to operationally evaluate air-launched guided missiles and their related systems, and to establish the techniques and procedures which would give the fleet the maximum utilization of an aircraft and its given missle system.

The development of the Sparrow I missile became the first project for VX-4. As the Sparrow II emerged, so did the Demon. From then on the F3H-2M and F3H-2 (later F-3C and F-3B respectively) would be common sights in the skys above Pt. Mugu until the ened of the 60's.

Pt. Mugu also became active in helping to convert fleet Demons into Sparrow III capable aircraft.

PHOTOS: TOP — F3H-2M, 133632, of VX-4, in flight on 2-2-57 with Sparrow I missiles. USN via Wyckoff. MIDDLE — VX-4 Demon, 143428, armed with Sparrow III missiles on the deck of CVA-41 in late 1957. USN Tailhook photo. BOTTOM — 143428 again on 8-22-58 without the fin tip colors as seen above. Note black painted area behind oil vent on rear fuselage. USN via Wyckoff.

PHOTOS: TOP — F3H-2, 143428, again with a new nose number at a NAS Miramar open house on 9-12-59, by W. Swisher. MIDDLE — F3H-2, 143422, armed with Sparrow IIIs and Sidewinders on 5-16-59 at NAS Pt. Magu air show, notice open gun door. Swisher photo. BOTTOM — VX-4 F3H-2, 143430, banks away from camera on 12-3-59, while hunting KDA targets during the Naval Air Weapons Meet.

VX-3 PHOTO ABOVE — F3H-2N, 133579, from VX-3 on 5-60 via W.T. Larkins. Note Demon carried starter pod on ground.

VF(AW)3

VF(AW)3 was originally activated as NACTUPAC on 22 Aug. 1944. Then based at NAS Barbers Point, the squadrons mission was to provide night combat training for Pacific coast pilots.

On 6 April 1946, the squadron started a series of name changes, culminating in VF(AW)3. These designation were: 6 April 1946 — Night DevRon Pac., 15 Nov. 1946 — VCN-1, 1 Aug. 1948 — FAWTUPAC and 2 May 1958 — VF(AW)3.

After the war the squadron's mission changed to that of an all-weather training squadron. AS FAWTUPAC from 27 Oct. 1953 to 2 May 1958, they maintained Detachment Bravo at NAS Moffett Field. In Feb. 1955, FAWTUPAC transferred its home base to NAS North Island, Calif. Also in 1955 FAWTU PAC was given the job of supplementing the Air Forces Air Defense program.

VF(AW)3 flew the F3D Skynight, F4D Skyray and the F3H Demon.

VC-3

Grey Knight with black markings and book. Red V. Light blue shield on dark blue field. White boarder with black lettering.

VC-3 was commissioned on 20 May 1949 at San Diego, Calif. Then on 27 Sept. 1949, the squadron relocated to NAS Moffett Field, Calif. The squadrons mission was to train fleet replacement pilots and maintenance personnel and to provide Fleet instrument training. In this capacity VC-3 acquired the Demon. VC-3 merged with VF(AW)3 on 1 July 1956.

PHOTO BELOW — F3H-2N of VC-3 on 5-56 in grey and white scheme with blue wing pylons and red interior gear doors and silver gear. W.T. Larkins photo.

PHOTOS: TOP — Two F3H-2N Demons of VC-3 over San Diego on 5-12-56. ABOVE — Four VC-3 Demons returning to NAS North Island on 5-12-56. Note location of wing codes. NA photos. BELOW — F3H-2N, 133583, of VC-3 with blue tail stripe and white stars. 5-56 photo by Larkins. BOTTOM — F3H-2N, 133581, of VFAW-3 on 9-56. Note silver gear and red interior gear doors. Larkins photo.

VF-13 "AGGRESSORS"

The "AGRESSORS" were commissioned in Sept. 1948 by taking personnel and aircraft from two other squadrons in Carrier Air Group One. These squadrons were VF-11 and VF-12, whose insignias were incorporated into VF-13's patch.

VF-13 flew the F4D-1 Skyray from Jan. 1959 until Sept. 1962, when the venerable Ford was replaced by the F3H Demon.

On 14 Sept. 1962, VF-13 started receiving Demons as it started absorbing personnel and aircraft from VF-131 which was decommissioned on 30 Sept. 1962. On 15 Oct., CDR Tully took his squadron aboard the USS Independence (CVA-62). The Caribbean cruise lasted through 23 Nov., during which time the ship and squadron took part in the blockade of Cuba. At Mayport, VF-13 embarked in the USS Lexington (CVS-16) from 24 Nov. to 7 Dec. 1962. The period between 7 Dec. 1962 and 28 March 1963 would find VF-13 homeported at NAS Cecil Field. After that date the squadron would go aboard the USS Shangri La (CVA-38) for her shakedown cruise in the Caribbean. This first cruise would last until 25 May. Four other deployments aboard CVA-38 would occur in 1963. They were; 16 June to 26 July, 25 Aug. to 6 Sept., 19 Sept. until 30 Sept. and on 1 Oct. 1963, the Shangri La

deployed to the Mediterranean until 25 May 1964. VF-13 was the last Demon squadron in the Atlantic fleet, with the F8U Crusader taking over on 2 July 1964. By Sept., the transition to the F-8E was complete. In Aug. of 1969, while still flying Crusaders, VF-13 was decommissioned at NAS Oceana.

PHOTO BELOW— F3B, 145240, of VF-13, loading on board the USS Shangri-La (CVA-38) on 8-23-63. Tail band is red with white stars. USN photo.

Two more USN photos showing VF-13 Demons being loaded on CVA-38, note the use of only one belly tank. Note red fuselage stripe and white boarder around AK on the tail. Also note only two cannons are installed.

CDR Tully, CO of VF-13 stands next to the nose gear of 143412 on 1-1-63. Photo shows off nose area detail and gives a good idea to the size of the beast. Note the upper cannons have been removed and the gun ports have been covered over. USN photo.

PHOTOS: TOP — VF-13, F3B 146715 and 143492 in flight on 2-27-63. Note short beaver tail and retrofitted fin tip beacon. USN photo. ABOVE — VF-13, 143412, at NAF Litchfield Park on 3-18-63. Refueling probe is black, Swisher photo.

AT RIGHT — VF-13, F3B, 145221, at Pima Co. Air Museum on 9-12-74. D. Spering photo. Photo shows ass-end view of the short beaver tail to good advantage. Also note wing spoiler.

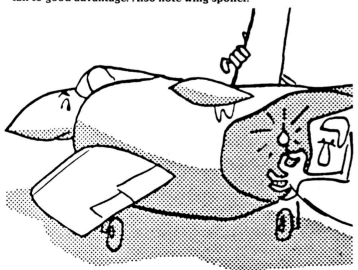

VF-14 'TOP HATTERS'

WORLD'S FIRST AND FOREMOST

The slogan above results from the fact that Fighter Squadron Fourteen was the U.S. Navy's first fighter squadron. The squadron started out in Sept. 1919 as Air Detachment, Pacific Fleet, based at NAS San Diego. An element of the squadron became VT-5 on 15 June 1920. The squadron became VP-4-1 in Sept. 1921. It then became Combat Squadron Four and was deactivated from Dec. 1921 until May of 1922. It was designated VF-1 on 1 July 1922, then VF-1B on 1 July 1927, then VB-2B on 1 July 1934, then VB-3 on 1 July 1937, then VB-4 on 1 July 1939, then VS-41 on 15 March 1941, then VB-41 on 1 March 1943, then VB-4 on 4 Aug. 1943, then VA-1A on 15 Nov. 1946, then VA-14 on 2 Aug. 1948 and finally VF-14 on 19 Dec. 1949.

The aircraft flown by the 'Top Hatters' were the following; Martin MBT-1, Curtiss R6L, Vought VE-7, Naval Aircraft Factory TS-1, Boeing FB-5, F2B and F3B, Curtiss F8C and F11C, SB2U Vindicator, F4F and FM2 Wildcats, SBD Dauntless, SB2C Helldiver, F4U Corsair, F3D Skyknight, F3H Demon, F-4 Phantom and the F-14 Tomcat.

VF-14 traded its Skyknights for the F3H-2N Demon in March of 1956, which made it the first fleet unit to equip with the F3H. Flying from Cecil Field as part of CVG-1 untill replaced by the F-4 Phantom in May of 1963. The squadron deployed on a short shake down cruise in 1957 while aboard the USS Forrestal (CVA-59) in 1957. Four further cruises would be made by VF-14, all aboard the USS Franklin D. Roosevelt (CVA-42). These cruises took place in 1957, 1958-59, 1960, 1961 and 1962-63.

HARRY MILNER REMEMBERS VF—14

As related earlier, I started flying the Demon with VF-14 in Feb. of 1958, and in June went to Point Mugu with six aircraft for Sparrow III installation. When we returned, we proceeded to learn the finer points of flying the airplane. These included inflight refueling, and squadron cross country navigation as well as dog fighting and intercepts.

By Feb. of 1959, we had left on our cruise. By this time the airplane had been redesignated F3H-2. We still had a few F3H-2Ms in the squadron, but these were not Sparrow III capable like the F3H-2s, and therefore did not go on the cruise.

We had three sets of airplanes on our cruises; one set for workup, a new set for the first cruise, replacement aircraft for the second cruise as ours were in rework, and the reworked aircraft on the third cruise.

As mentioned earlier in the book, VF-14 had received the coveted safety award and Battle "E" three years in a row, 1959-60-61. One of the factors that allowed us to accomplish this historical feat was the fact that the personnel assigned to the squadron remained unchanged from Nov. of 1957 till our third cruise in 1961. This allowed us to become a successful team.

FIGHTER SQUADRON FOURTEEN

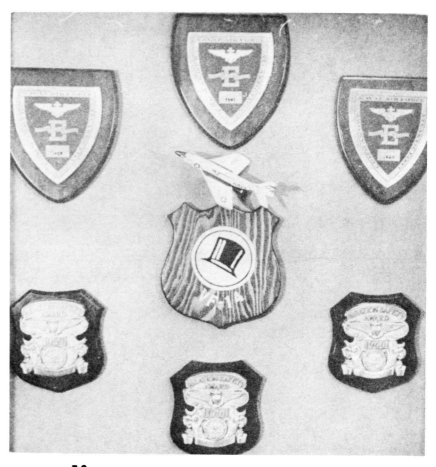

ABOVE — Photo of VF-14 patch, colors are black on white. **AT RIGHT** — Photo of VF-14 awards for 1959, 1960 and 1961, the coveted safety award and Battle "E" for three years in a row. Photo via Harry Milner.

PHOTO ABOVE — Early photo of VF-14 F3H-2N Demons. Bottom is factory fresh 133596 before markings were applied. Above it is 133593 with the 1956 T tail code. Top two 133567 and 144565 have the added red fin stripes. BOTTOM PHOTO — F3H-2N, 133591, on the elevator of the Forrestal (CVA-59) on 9-26-56. Note wing codes and red fin and wing tip stripes. MDC photos.

COLOR PLATES – TOP — VF-41, F3H-2, 143449, a Naval Weapons Meet MCASS Yuma on 12-3-59. MIDDLE — VF-151, F3B, 146735, at NAS Miramar on 1-19-63. BOTTOM — VF-13, F3B, F3B, 143487, at NAF Litchfield Park on 3-18-63. Photos by Swisher.

PHOTOS: VF-14 F3H-2Ns 133588, 133593, and 133592 on the forward deck of CVA-59 with three A3 Skywarriors. Note second red wing tip stripe does not continue on the bottom of the wing, also note black aircraft numbers are painted on the top red fin stripe. 9-25-56 MDC photo. MIDDLE — F3H-2N, 133593, pulls forward on CVA-59 on 9-26-56. BOTTOM — Unexplained photo of VF-14 F3H-2N, 133594, with Marine on the fuselage. Was the plane zapped or was it a demonstration aircraft. MDC photos.

PHOTOS: TOP — Three VF-14 Demons with another new paint scheme. 2-17-57 photo with 1956 T tail code. Note white I.D. numbers on upper red fin stripe, also note red fuselage flash with top-hat insignia in center. MDC photo. MIDDLE — Forward deck of the USS Franklin D. Roosevelt during its 1958-59 cruise with eleven of VF-14 Demons. Note new tail markings. USN via H. Milner. BELOW — 4-3-61 photo of VF-14 F3H-2, 145221, being refueled by VA-172 A4D-2, 142697. USN photo.

The deck of the USS Ranger in Aug. 1961 with eight VF-92 Demons in view. W.T. Larkins photo.

ABOVE — VF-14, F3H-2, 145288, on starboard catapult aboard the USS Roosevelt (CVA-41) on 6-20-61. BELOW — VF-31, F3H-2, 145224, on 5-27-60 USN photos.

PHOTO ABOVE — 1961 photo of VF-14 Demons being launched. Note single drop tank on the right side and USS Roosevelt on the side of the fuselage. PHOTO BELOW — F3H-2, 145287, on the port catapult of CVA-42 on 6-20-61. Note pilots excellent forward and that the upper cannons have been removed. USN photos.

PHOTOS — Two 1-23-63 photos of VF-14 Demons recovering aboard CVA-42 while deployed in the Mediterranean. Note single right side fuselage drop tank. USN photos.

F3H DEMON DEPLOYMENTS

YEAR	SQUAD.	CODES	SHIP	AIR GROUP	AREA
1957	VF-14	100/T	CVA-59	CVG-1	MED
1957	VF-124	200/D	CVA-16	CVG-12	W.P.
1957/58	VF-122	400/NG	CVA-14	CVG-9	W.P.
1958	VF-24	100/NP	CVA-16	CVG-21	W.P.
1958	VF-114	400/NH	CVA-38	CVG-11	W.P.
1958	VF-31	100/AC	CVA-60	CVG-3	MED
1958/59	VF-112	100/NA	CVA-14	ATG-1	W.P.
1958/59	VF-193	300/NM	CVA-31	CVG-19	W.P.
1958/59	VF-64	200/NE	CVA-41	CVG-2	W.P.
1959	VF-114	400/NH	CVA-38	CVG-11	W.P.
1959	VF-14	100/AB	CVA-42	CVG-1	MED
1959/60	VF-151	100/NL	CVA-19	CVG-15	W.P.
1959/60	VF-193	300/NM	CVA-31	CVG-19	W.P.
1959/60	VF-21	200/NE	CVA-41	CVG-2	W.P.
1959/60	VF-31	100/AC	CVA-60	CVG-3	MED
1960	VF-53	200/NF	CVA-14	CVG-5	W.P.
1960	VF-141	200/NK	CVA-34	CVG-14	W.P.
1960	VF-14	100/AB	CVA-42	CVG-1	MED
1960	VF-92	200/NG	CVA-61	CVG-9	W.P.
1960/61	VF-213	300/NP	CVA-16	CVG-21	W.P.
1960/61	VF-114	400/NH	CVA-19	CVG-11	W.P.
1960/61	VF-151	100/NL	CVA-43	CVG-15	W.P.
1960/61	VF-31	100/AC	CVA-60	CVG-3	MED
1960/61	VF-41	100/AG	CVA-62	CVG-7	MED
1961	VF-193	300/NM	CVA-31	CVG-19	W.P.
1961	VF-21	200/NE	CVA-41	CVG-2	W.P.
1961	VF-14	100/AB	CVA-42	CVG-1	MED
1961	VF-41	100/AG	CVA-62	CVG-7	MED
1961/62	VF-53	200/NF	CVA-14	CVG-5	W.P.
1961/62	VF-141	100/NK	CVA-16	CVG-14	W.P.
1961/62	VF-151	100/NL	CVA-43	CVG-15	W.P.
1961/62	VF-31	100/AC	CVA-60	CVG-3	MED
1961/62	VF-92	200/NG	CVA-61	CVG-9	W.P.
1962	VF-213	300/NP	CVA-19	CVG-21	W.P.
1962	VF-161	100/AH	CVA-34	CVG-16	W.P.
1962	VF-21	200/NE	CVA-41	CVG-2	W.P.
1962	VF-131	100/AE	CVA-64	CVG-13	S.D.
1962/63	VF-193	300/NM	CVA-31	CVG-19	W.P.
1962/63	VF-14	100/AB	CVA-42	CVG-1	MED
1963	VF-54	200/NF	CVA-14	CVG-5	W.P.
1963	VF-213	300/NP	CVA-19	CVG-21	W.P.
1963	VF-151	100/NL	CVA-43	CVG-15	W.P.
1963	VF-31	100/AC	CVA-60	CVG-3	MED
1963/64	VF-161	100/AH	CVA-34	CVG-16	W.P.
1963/64	VF-13	100/AK	CVA-38	CVG-11	W.P.

S.D. = SHAKEDOWN

PHOTO BELOW — VF-112, Demon, 137050, D. Spering photo.

BLOCK LETTERS

143433n BuAer SERIAL NUMBER
n BLOCK DESIGNATION LETTER

F3H-2
NAVY
143433n

BLOCK d (4)
F3H-2   133549d thru 133568d
F3H-2   133570d thru 133578d
F3H-2M 133569d*

BLOCK e (5)
F3H-2   133579e thru 133603e
F3H-2M 133623e thru 133627e

BLOCK f (6)
F3H-2   133604f thru 133622f
F3H-2M 133628f thru 133638f

BLOCK g (7)
F3H-2   136966g thru 136982g
F3H-2M 137033g thru 137040g

BLOCK h (8)
F3H-2   136983h thru 137012h*

BLOCK i (9)
F3H-2   137013i thru 137020i
F3H-2M 137041i thru 137062i

BLOCK j (10)
F3H-2   137021j thru 137030j
F3H-2M 137063j thru 137082j

BLOCK k (11)
F3H-2   137031k and 137032k
F3H-2M 137083k thru 137095k

BLOCK m (12)
F3H-2 143403m thru 143432m

BLOCK n (13)
F3H-2 143433n thru 143462n

BLOCK o (14)
F3H-2 143463o thru 143492o

BLOCK p (15)
F3H-2 145202p thru 145231p

BLOCK q (16)
F3H-2 145232q thru 145261q

BLOCK r (17)
F3H-2 145262r thru 145291r

BLOCK s (18)
F3H-2 145292s thru 145306s
F3H-2 146328s thru 146339s

BLOCK t (19)
F3H-2 146709t thru 146740t

*DENOTES PROTOTYPE

COLOR SECTION

1. F3H-1N, 133491, blue overall, natural metal leading edges, inside gear doors red, by Balogh via Menard. 2. F3H-2N, 133555, VF-114, on 3-60, at NAS North Island, by Jansson. 3. F3H-2, 133572 and sister, VF-131, on board USS CONSTELLATION, on 1-62, by Manufacturer. 4. F3H-2, 143428, VF-161, at NAS Miramar, on 1-63, by Jansson. 5. VF-213 line at NAS Miramar on 1-63, with 146733 in foreground, by Jansson. 6. F3H-2, 143449, VF-41, Picciani Aircraft Slides. 7. F3H-2M, 3637, VF-61, via Williams. 8. Prototype XF3H-1 Demon during carrier suitability trials, by Manufacturer. 9. F3H-2N, 137016, VF-82, by Parmerter via Menard. 10. F3H, 143457, VF-193, with faded blue markings, by Jansson. 11. F3H-2, 145257, VF-121, at NAS Miramar, on 7-60, by Jansson.

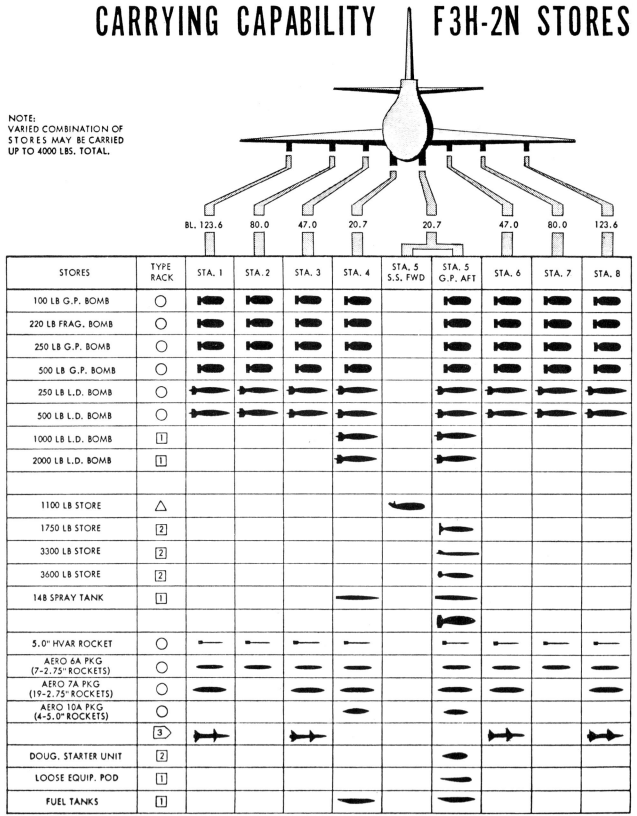

PHOTO ABOVE — F3B, 145281, of VF-14 goes over the bow of CVA-42 on 3-20-63, pilot was Lt. J.G. Joseph Janiak, Jr., fate unknown. Note wing code of Demon in the foreground. USN photo. PHOTO BELOW — Poor photo of VAH-15 AJ Savage with four VF-14 Demons awaiting their turn at the pump. USN via H. Milner.

PHOTOS: TOP — VF-14 F3B, 145290, lands on F.D.R. on 4-23-63 during its Med cruise. USN photo. AT RIGHT — The end of the line for this VF-14 F3H-2, 133587. At NAF Litchfield Park on 3-18-63, photo by Swisher. Latin phrase under AB code is PRIMUS PRINCIPES. BELOW — Photo of three McDonnell Naval fighters on 8-3-63 showing a Canadian F2H-3 Banshee, a VF-14 F3B Demon and VF-101 F4B 158432. USN photo.

VF-14 'TOP HATTERS'

WORLD'S FIRST AND FOREMOST

VF-21 'FREELANCERS'

Fighter squadron twenty-one was originally commissioned on 1 March 1944 at NAS Atlantic City, N.J. as VF-81. The squadron then was redesignated VF-13A on 15 Nov. 1946, VF-131 on 2 Aug. 1948, VF-64 on 1 Dec. 1949 and finally VF-21, on 1 July 1959.

The Freelancers have flown the F6F Hellcat, F8F Bearcat, F4U Corsair, F9F Panther, F2H Banshee, F3H Demon, F-4 Phantom and the F-14 Tomcat. The squadron flew the Demon while designated VF-64 and VF-21. In Sept. of 1962, VF-21 turned in their Demons for F4B Phantoms and reported to VF-121 for transition training.

While equipped with the Demon, VF-21 deployed three times aboard USS Midway as part of CVW-2. These deployments were in 1959-60, 1961 and 1962. Between 1961 and 1962 VF-21 moved to NAS Miramar.

Black cat, black and white shield, green lettering, green stripes under cats paws, yellow background.

PHOTOS BELOW — First two photos in a series showing F3H-2, 143435, of VF-21 making a barrier landing on the USS Midway (CVA-41) on 4-28-62. USN photos. Colors are gull-grey and white with yellow fin-tip, rudder stripes, wing-tips and horizontal tail-tips. Area behind squadron emblem on fuselage is yellow. Fuselage stripe is black. Note location of wing codes, and the #3 on the beaver tail

PHOTO ABOVE — Two VF-21 F3H-2 Demons, 145283 and 145268, over the ocean in 1962. USN/Tailhook photo.

VF-24 'CORSAIRS'

Originally commissioned as VB-74 on 1 May 1945, then VA-1B on 15 Nov. 1946, then VA-24 on 1 Sept. 1948, then VF-24 on 1 Dec. 1949 and finally VF-211 on 9 March 1959 when VF-24 and VF-211 switched squadron designations in order to properly align the squadron designations with the air group to which they were assigned.

VF-24 received its first F3H-2M Demons in the summer of 1957, and as part of CVG-21 deployed the F3H from 16 July 1958 until 19 Dec. 1958. Three days after their return to NAS Moffett Field the squadron started receiving F11F-1 Tigers.

Aircraft-wise the squadron flew the SBC Helldiver, the A-1 Skyraider, the F4U Corsair, the F9F Panther, the F9F Cougar, the FJ-3 Fury, the F3H Demon, the F11F Tiger, the F8 Crusader and the F-14 Tomcat.

PHOTO BELOW — Partial side view of VF-24 F3H-2M on 5-58. Fuselage stripe and Corsair hat red, eye patch and VF-24 black. Note dark blue Sparrow I and rocket rail.

PHOTO ABOVE — VF-24, F3H-2M, 137088, on 9-57 with original CVG-2 NE tail code. Note white area on tail that shows the extent of the horizontal tails travel. Note interior of speed brake is red. W.T. Larkins photos. PHOTO BELOW — Three VF-24 Demons 137072, 137069 and 137070 on board the USS Lexington (CVA-16) while passing below the Golden Gate bridge on 7-7-58. Note CVG-21 tail code. Fuselage and tail stripes are red. W.T. Larkins photo. Note CVG-16 NP tail code.

VF-31 'TOMCATTERS'

ALIAS FELIX THE CAT

Fighter Squadron Thirty One started life as VF-1B, then it became VF-6B, then VF-3, then VF-3A and finally VF-31 on 7 Aug. 1948.

Aircraft flown by the squadron were the Boeing F4B-4, the Grumman FF-1, SF-1 and F3F, the F2A Buffalo, the F4F Wildcat, the F6F Hellcat, the F8F Bearcat, the F9F Panther, the F2H Banshee, the F3H Demon, the F-4 Phantom and finally todays F-14 Tomcat.

Transition to the F3H Demon began in 1956 while stationed at NAS Cecil Field. VF-31 deployed its Demons five times aboard the USS Saratoga (CVA-60) before being replaced by F-4's in Oct. of 1963. During their 1958 cruise they participated in operations during the Lebanon crisis. And in Dec. 1962 along with other elements of CVG-3 from the Saratoga, flew combat air patrols during the Cuban blockade. The last cruise started in May 1963 and ended in Oct.

Black and white Felix on a yellow background red flames on fuse.

PHOTOS: TOP — VF-31 Demon 136993 on 9-16-58. MDC photo. Fin-tip, fuselage flash and wing tip are red. Aircraft still has 1956 K tailcode. Black Felix on a yellow circle above K. **BOTTOM** — VF-31 Demon refuels from A-1 Skyraider 137547 while over the Med. USN

91

PHOTOS: TOP — VF-31, F3H-2N, 137018, in the same markings as 136993 on the previous page except the 1956 K has been replaced by a black AC with a thin white outline on a wide red tail stripe. Photo via S. Nicolaou. MIDDLE — Another change of markings on VF-31 Demon 145224. Red fuselage flash has been deleted and Felix has been added with four black stars behind him. VA-36 A4D 142895 refuels VA-34 A4D 144891 which refuels the VF-31 F3H. BOTTOM — Another change of markings on VF-31 F3H 143414. Red fin-tip has been deleted and a new red chevron with Felix in the middle was added on the fuselage. Note battle E single drop tank, Sidewinder and Sparrow IIIminus fins. Note upper two cannons have been deleted. 2-19-63 USN photo.

PHOTO ABOVE — Four VF-31 Demons, 143488, 143476, 145299 and 143486 over the Med in 1962. PHOTO BELOW — F3B Demons 143476, 145299, 145245 and 143405 over the USS Saratoga (CVA-60) on 4-62. USN photos.

PHOTOS: TOP — Flight deck activity aboard the USS Saratoga (CVA-60) on 13 April 1962. USN photo. AT RIGHT — VF-31 F3B, 143488, at the end of its life at NAF Litchfield Park on 3-18-63. Note white rudder, photo by Swisher. BOTTOM — VF-31 F3B, 145239, tensioned on a H-8 catapault, at NAS Patuxent River, Md. Note red area under slats and a short beaver tail. USN photo.

VF-31 'TOMCATTERS'

FELIX THE CAT

94

VF-41 'BLACK ACES'

The Black Aces started out life as VF-75 on 1 June 1945 at NAAS Chincoteaque, Virginia. They flew the F4U Corsair and moved to NAS Norfolk in 1947. In Nov. 1946 they became VF-3B and in Sept. 1948 VF-41. They moved to NAS Jacksonville in Jan. 1949 and were decommissioned for a short period in early 1950 and then recommissioned at NAS Oceana. The squadron flew the F2H Banshee from 1953 to 1958 when it was replaced by the F3H Demon. The Demon was replaced by its offspring the F-4 Phantom in Feb. 1962 and then the F-14 Tomcat in April 1976.

While flying the Demon VF-41 distinguished itself as the best all weather fighter squadron by winning the Topgun award at the Naval Weapons Meet in 1959 at Yuma. The squadron spent most of 1959 and early 1960 in a series of shakedown trials aboard the newly commissioned USS Independence (CVA-62). They finally deployed from Aug. 1960 to March 1961 on a cruise to the Med. as part of CVG-7.

Black and yellow cloud and and red below patch with white lower body stripe Ace.

PHOTOS: Two USN photos of VF-41 Demons with ATG-181 AM tailcodes while operating off the USS Intrepid in May of 1958. Top 143483 via D. Spering. Bottom 143437 via Lt. Col. Miller. Tail stripes are red and black.

PHOTOS: TOP — F3H-2, 143449, in VF-41 CVG-7 AG tailcode at Lakehurst. O'Dell via W.T. Larkins. Tail stripes are red. Fuselage stripe is red with a black outline. Names under canopy are CDR H C MAC KNIGHT AND MURPHY J W ADJ3. MIDDLE — Same aircraft sharing the blimp hangar with a EC-121J assigned to the Naval Air Development Unit. Via S. Nicolaou. BOTTOM — VF-41 F3H-2, 143436, with Lt. R.P. JOHN and KRUEGEN J.F. ADJ3 under the canopy. Note two rocket racks and one bomb rack. Via Larkins.

PHOTOS: TOP — VF-41 CAG Bird as it appeared when the squadron won the Topgun award at the Naval Weapons Meet at MCASS Yuma 12-3-59. Swisher photo. Tail colors from top to bottom are red, yellow, blue, orange, green and black. USS INDEPENDENCE is in orange. MIDDLE — Two VF-41 F3H Demons over the Med on 10-11-61. USN photo. Tail stripes on 145239 are top to bottom; red, red, orange, red, orange, red and orange. 146716 has all red tail stripes. BOTTOM — VF-41 F3H-2, 143487, in flight with Sparrow III and Sidewinder on 10-10-61. USN photo. Note faded radome.

PHOTO ABOVE — May 1959 photo of the USS Independence (CVA-62) refueling the USS Manley DD-940 with seven VF-41 Demons on the forward deck. USN photo. PHOTO BELOW — VF-41 F3H doing touch-and-goes aboard CVA-62 on 12-13-60. Note fully extended length of the nose gear. USN photos.

PHOTOS: TOP — Good belly view of VF-41 Demon. 10-10-61 USN photo shows Sidewinders, Sparrows and one belly tank. MIDDLE — VF-41 F3H-2, 145246, launches off CVA-62 during operation Riptide in the Atlantic on 7-61. BOTTOM — 146716 recovers on CVA-62 on 10-61. Note white has been added between the tail stripes. USN photos.

VF-53

Fighting Squadron Fifty Three was originally commissioned as an NAS Alameda reserve squadron, VF-871, in 1949. The squadron used the F4U Corsair until 1953 when they acquired the F9F Panther and the designation VF-123. VF-123 received the F9F Cougar in 1956. In 1958 the squadron received the F3H Demon and the designation VF-53. VF-53 took the Demon on two cruises in 1960 and 1961 while aboard the USS Ticonderoga (CVA-14). On 20 June 1962, VF-53 was redesignated VF-143 and reequipped with the F-4 Phantom. Today VF-143 flies the F-14A Tomcat.

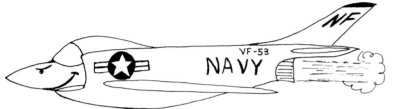

PHOTOS: AT RIGHT — VF-53 patch, lettering outlines and pukin dog black, grey shield with three white stripes at top and white background for BLUE KNIGHTS. BELOW — Four VF-53 F3H-2 Demons over NAS North Island on 11-20-60. Fin tips are yellow with either white or black numbers. 143467, 143427 and 145304 all have NF tail code on top edge of fin and small VF-53 fuselage as well as the last four digits of the Buro No. 145264 has NF on the rudder and large VF-53 and numbers on the fin. USN photos.

PHOTOS: TOP — VF-53 F3H-2, 145303, at MCAAS YUMA on 12-3-59 for the Naval Weapons Meet. Swisher photo. Fin tip is yellow with white number 8. BOTTOM — Four unarmed VF-53 Demons peel off on 11-20-60. USN photo.

VF-54 'SILVER KINGS'

See VF-92 section.

PHOTOS: TOP — VF-54 F3H2, 136985, on deaths row on 3-23-63. Swisher photo. MIDDLE — Two VF-54 F3H's, 145213 and 143440 from the USS Ticonderoga (CVA-14) on 2-5-63. Fin tip is yellow with a thin black boarder and red chessman. BOTTOM — 143440 again with 145271 on 4-63. USN photos.

VF-61 received their first Demons in Sept. 1956, and were homeported at NAS Oceana, Virginia. During 1957 the squadron participated in many Fleet and NATO exercises. The "Jolly Rogers" were aboard the USS Franklin D. Roosevelt (CVA-42) from April 6th to the 15th. Then, on 11 May, they embarked aboard the USS Saratoga (CVA-60) until returning to NAS Oceana on June 9th. During 6 and 7 June, VF-61 participated in LANTFLEX 1-57, which demonstrated air-to-surface rocket fire, in-flight refueling and combat air patrol to the president and selected cabinet members. The squadron deployed to CVA-60 from 8 Aug. to 22 Oct. of 1957. During this period they participated in Task Group 28 operations and operations "Intex", "Sea Spray" and "Strike Back". The last operation aboard Saratoga was operation "Pipe Down" from Oct 13th to 16th. This was a NATO operation in which VF-61 became the first Demon squadron to land aboard the HMS Ark Royal. 3 Nov. to 14 Nov. found the squadron aboard CVA-59. A short six day stint aboard the USS Forrestal (CVA-59) from 20 Nov. to 25 Nov. ended VF-61's at sea periods in 1957.

In 1958 the "Jolly Rogers" did not register any at sea time and operated from its home port of NAS Oceana for the entire year, except for a short stint at NAS Roosevelt Roads, Puerto Rico, from 4 Nov. to 12 Nov. 1958. During 1958, VF-61 participated in many Fleet exercises. One pioneer operation was "Pipeline." In this operation, Det A supplied 4 F3H-2N replacement aircraft to the Sixth Fleet at Port Lyautey, French Moraco. This May operation was so successful that it was repeated in Aug., when aircraft were ferried to Naples.

In 1959 the squadron was slated to receive the F8U-2 Crusader, but instead was decommissioned on 15 April 1959. In June of 1959, VF-84 took over the "Jolly Roger" name and insignia, their previous designation was "Vagabonds."

BLACK FLAG WITH WHITE SKULL AND CROSSBONES AND BOARDERS

VF-61 "JOLLY ROGERS"

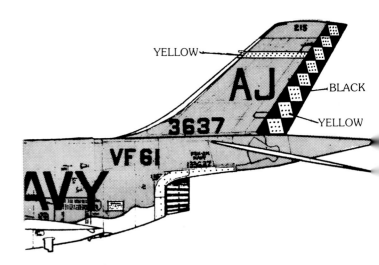

TAIL CODE DRAWING ABOVE ILLUSTRATES THE CVG-8 TAIL CODE AJ USED ON VF-61 AIRCRAFT IN LATE 1958 AND EARLY 1959. SEE COLOR SECTION FOR PHOTO OF THIS AIRCRAFT.

PHOTO BELOW — F3H-2M of VF-61 on board ship in April of 1957 with E tail code. MDC photo.

PHOTOS: TOP — F3H-2M, 137036, doing a touch-and-go on board the USS Saratoga (CVA-60) in 1957. Plane still carries the single L CVG-7 tail code. USN/Tailhook photo. MIDDLE — F3H-2M, 133638, lands on CVA-60, on 4-57. This Demon has the CVG-8 E tail code. BOTTOM — F3H-2M, 133633, doing a touch-and-go on CVA-60, tail and rear canopy markings are black and yellow. MDC photo 4-57.

PHOTO ABOVE — F3H-2M, 133636, on 4-57 on board CVA-60, note silver landing gear, non-standard position of red rescue arrow, and red and white candy-striped fuel dump on trailing edge of wing. MDC photo. PHOTO BELOW — Poor quality Feb. 1958 photo of four VF-61 Demons in flight. Note CVG-7 AG tail code, yellow and black diamonds on rudder and wing-tips and horizontal stabilizer tips and rear cockpit edge, and all white horizontal stabilizer. Photo via Bob Bradus.

VF-64 'FREELANCERS'

VF-64 flew Demons from 1958 to 1959. The squadron deployed aboard the USS Midway (CVA-41) during the 1958-59 cruise. On 1 July 1959 the squadrons designation changed to VF-21. See VF-21 for more details.

PHOTOS: TOP — VF-64 F3H-2, 143410, in early CVG-2 markings on 5-58. W.T. Larkins photo. Note yellow tail stripes and black Freelancer cat. Intake covers are red. BOTTOM — Two VF-64 Demons, 145205 and 133457 on 1-2-59 over Japan. Markings are a black fuselage flash with the Freelancer patch on a yellow circle, wing tips are yellow, rudder is white and yellow stripes. Note wing codes. USN/Tailhook photo.
BELOW F3H-2 being refueled from AJ Savage USN/Tailhook

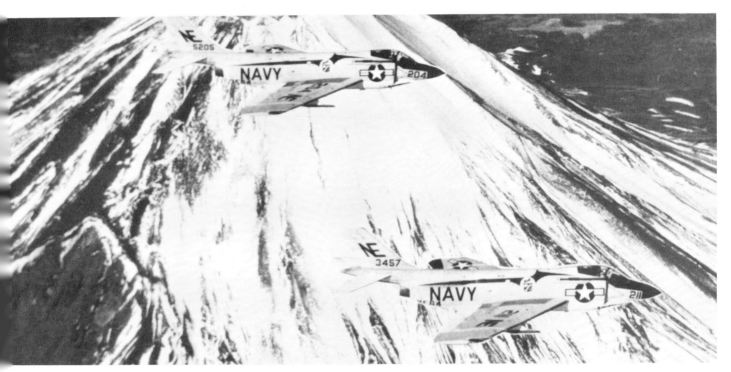

launched off the USS Midway (CVA-41) in Jan. 1959. USN photo.

Tailhook Association
Box 40
Bonita, CA 92002

VF-82 IRON MEN

Activated from reserve squadron VF-742 in February 1951, then stationed at NAS Jacksonville, VF-82 flew Panthers and Corsairs. The Iron Mens next mount would be the F2H Banshee, which was flown from NAS Oceana. After a cruise on the USS Intrepid (CVA-11), VF-82 traded in their Banshees for F3H Demons. The Iron Men flew Demons from 1956 to 1958.

Early E tail code at right with red and white rudder diamonds, see color section for photo.

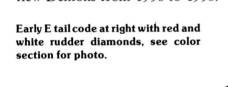

PHOTO BELOW — VF-82 F3H-2N, 133593, with AJ tail code, normal white and red checked rudder is missing and fin tip is red.

VF-92 'SILVER KINGS'

Motto, 'Death, Terror, and Vengeance.'

Fighter Squadron Ninety Two was commissioned at NAS Alameda on 26 March 1952. It started out flying the F4U Corsair, then the F9F-2 Panther in 1953, the AD-4 Skyraider in 1955, the F9F-5 Panther in 1956, the F2H-3 Banshee in Oct. 1956, the F3H Demon in May of 1959 and the F-4 Phantom in Aug. of 1963. The squadron ended its career flying the Phantom in 1975.

While part of CVG-9, VF-92 flew two cruises aboard the USS Ranger (CVA-61) in 1960 and 1961. Then the squadron was transferred to CVG-5 and the USS Lexington (CVA-16) in June/July of 1962. This transfer caused VF-92 to change its designation to VF-54. They returned from their 'Round the Horn' cruise by flying from the ship, cross country, to NAS Miramar in Sept. 1962. They then departed on board the USS Ticonderoga for a WESTPAC cruise from Jan. to July 1963. They were then redesignated VF-92 again in Oct. 1963.

White patch with black boarder, lettering, spade and snake markings, silver chessman, yellow snake with red mouth.

PHOTOS: TOP — First style VF-92 NG tail code on F3H-2, 145271, on 9-59. W.T. Larkins photo. Note unusual position of nose numbers 202 and yellow fin tip. BOTTOM — Second style VF-92 NG tail code on F3H-2, 143442, note faded radome and blue and white Sidewinder. Larkins photo.

PHOTOS: TOP — F3H-2, 143444, with yellow fin and wing tips. Larkins photo. MIDDLE — Two VF-92 Demons, 136987 and 137007 refuel from A3 Skywarrier 147655 belonging to VAH-6. USN/Tailhook photo. BOTTOM — VF-92 F3H-2, 133577, in Nov. 1962 while assigned to CVG-5 as denoted by NF tailcode. This was just prior to departing on the USS Ticonderoga in Jan. 1963. Fin tip is yellow H. Gann photo.

patch, red with black border and VF-101, Grim Reapers yellow, skeleton white.

PHOTO ABOVE — Demon Doctor Joel Griggs 2nd. from left. Co Capt. Hardy at left. CVA-62 in 1959.

VF-101 'GRIM REAPERS'

VF-10, the original Grim Reapers had the distinction of being the first fighter squadron to be commissioned after Pearl harbor, on 3 June 1943. During the war they flew the F4F Wildcat, then the F6F Hellcat and then the F4U Corsair.

The squadron was commissioned VF-101 on 1 May 1952 at NAS Cecil Field. They flew a mixed bag of F4U Corsairs and F2H-1 Banshees. They then flew F2H-2 and F2H-3 Banshee aircraft until replaced by the F4D-1 Skyray in Aug. 1956. In April 1958 the squadron moved to NAS Key West (Boca Chica) and became responsible for training replacement aircrews for the F4D-1 Skyray and F3H Demon. In this capacity the squadron flew the F3H Demon, the F4D Skyray, the F3D Skyknight, the TV-2 Shooting Star, the F9F-8T Cougar and a R4D Skytrain. By 1962 the Skyrays and Demons were replaced by the F-4 Phantom II and today they fly the F-14 Tomcat.

JOEL GRIGGS, A DEMON 'DOCTOR' HAD THIS TO SAY ABOUT VF—101 AND HER DEMONS.

There were many times that the squadron would send detachments aboard carriers out of either Norfolk, Virginia, or Mayport, Florida (also a common practice with the Skyrays). When this happened, I would ususaly go aboard to be in charge of the Plane Captains. I remember going aboard the USS Intrepid (CVA-11) once. Our big Demons were barely able to be handled aboard the old ship. One other memorable deployment was with the CO, Capt. Lew Hardy. This was in 1959 aboard the USS Independence (CVA-62).

My first encounter with the 'Screamin' Demon' was in the summer of 1958. I was going through 'A' school for ADJs (jet mechanics), at NATTC Memphis, Tenn. When I first saw the aircraft, I thought, what a hog! After pulling her engine in school, I hoped I would never have to work on this type of aircraft again (I had previously worked on FJ-2 Furys). The Demon's engine was removed by pulling it straight back out of the plane. This required you to clear an area twice the length of the F3H, which was hard to do on a crowded carrier hanger deck.

I subsequently received orders to report to VF-101. I had no idea that the engines I had heard the night I walked through the main gate at Boca Chica were thosee of the Demon. The squadron was working two and sometimes three shifts at thc time. I reported in the next morning and was assigned to the maintenance division and then the flight line. I was assigned to work with a fellow from Texas for a week before being assigned my own aircrat. Within two months, I was responsible for all 52 of the F3H Demons assigned to VF-101. Being an E-4, I had replaced an E-6 who was needed back in the maintenance shop. Needless to say I had my work cut out for me, but I was to find out that we had very few problems with the Demon. The biggest problem with the plane proved to be the hydraulics, its belly was always red to burnt red, from all the leaks.

As VF-101 was part of the U.S. Air Force's Air Defense Command, four aircraft were always on the hot pad for scrambling at a moments notice. Unlike VFAW-3 these aircraft were Demons instead of Skyrays. Pilots and crews who stood this duty were especially tense during the Cuban Missile Crisis.

PHOTOS: TOP — VF-101 line at Boca Chica Field Key West Fla. in 1959. Note F3D-2T2 Skyknights in foreground which had the F3H Demon radars installed. Joel Griggs photo. MIDDLE — VF-101 F3H, 143450, after main gear failure at NAS Cecil Field on 1-26-62. USN via H. Milner. BOTTOM — F3H-2, 146715, at NAS Key West on 3-23-60. Tail stripe is red with white stars. USN via Lt. Col. Miller.

PHOTOS: TOP — Two VF-101 Demons being launched OFF THE USS Independence (CVA-62) on 5-11-60. 145243 is on the no. 1 catapult. USN photo. MIDDLE — VF-101 F3H-2, 143491, in the hangar bay of CVA-62. Note the A-1 drop tanks hanging in the rafters. Joel Griggs photo. BOTTOM — 1960 USN photo of VF-101 F3H-2, 145299 in flight.

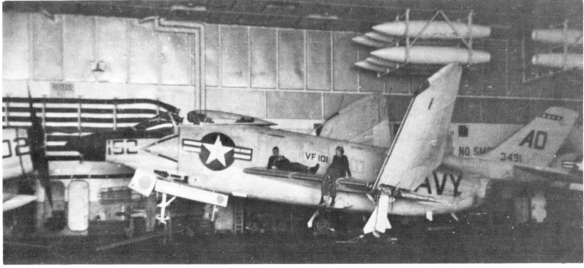

PHOTOS: TOP — VF-101 F3H-2, 143491, lands on board CVA-62 on 5-11-60. USN photo. ABOVE — VF-101 Skyray launches and a VF-101 Demon awaits. Tail stripe in red. Joel Griggs photo. AT LEFT — F3H-2 133557 at NAF Litchfield Park on 3-18-63, Swisher photo. BELOW — 133638. BOTTOM — F3H-2, 133598, on 3-18-63 via Jannson.

VF-112 was originally commissioned as VBF-11 on 9 April 1945 at NAS Alameda. It would then be redesignated VF-12A on 15 Nov. 1946, then VF-112 on 15 July 1948 and finally VA-112 on 23 Feb. 1959.

During its Demon years, winter 1956 to Feb. 1959, VF-112 would embark for brief periods aboard the USS Ticonderoga (CVA-14) from the squadrons home port of NAS Miramar. The squadron conducted its original carquals aboard the USS Midway (CVA-41) during March 9th to 15th, 1958. Refresher carquals were conducted aboard the USS Lexington (CVA-16), USS Kearsarge (CVA-33) and the USS Ticonderoga (CVA-14). The squadron deployed aboard the Tico- in Oct. 1958 for a West Pac cruise. Upon return to NAS Miramar the Demons were relinquished for FJ-4B Furys and the squadron was designated VA-112 and transferred to NAS Lemore, Calif.

Squadron patch — yellow field, blue upper shield, green lower shield, white stripe with red lettering, black boarders, bomb & Sword, gold & black wings, white dove with green leaves, grey helmet with red plume.

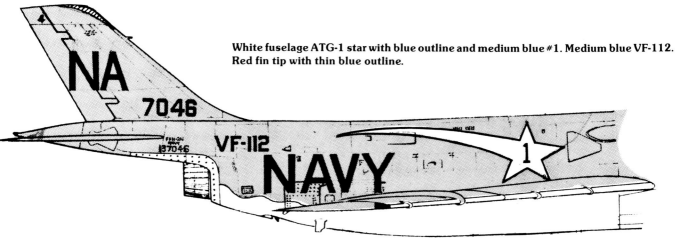

White fuselage ATG-1 star with blue outline and medium blue #1. Medium blue VF-112. Red fin tip with thin blue outline.

PHOTO BELOW — F3H of VF-112 after main gear failure at NAS Barbers Point Hawaii, note ATG-1 fuselage star and NA tail code. Tailhook photo.

PHOTO ABOVE — VF-112 flightline with F3H-2M 137056 in foreground. Although the aircraft carries a 200 series nose number, the tail fuselage and wing-tip marking are red. Note silver nose gear. Photo via Larkins. AT LEFT — Inflight view of F3H-2M, 137055. BELOW — F3H-2M, 137050, in Aug. 1957 at NAS Miramar. Larkins photo.

PHOTO BELOW — All blue F3H-2N of the Naval Air Technical Training Unit, AB/School, photo via R.F. Besecker.

"EXECUTIONERS" VF-114 'AARDVARKS'

Fighter Squadron One Hundred Fourteen began life as VF-5B on 2 July 1934, at NAS Norfolk. In July 1937 the squadron changed to the West Coast and was redesignated VB-2. VB-2 was decommissioned on 1 July 1942 and recommissioned as VB-11 on 10 Oct. 1942. On 15 Nov. 1945 VB-11 became VF-11 and then VA-11A in Nov. 1946. In July 1948 they became VA-114 and finally on 15 Feb. 1950, VF-114.

The squadron has flown the Boeing F4B-4, the BF2C-1, the SB2U, the SBD Dauntless, the SB2C Helldiver, the F4U Corsair, the F9F Panther, the F2H Banshee, the F3H Demon, the F-4 Phantom and the F-14 Tomcat.

The First Demon was received in 1957. 1961 would see VF-114 became the first Pacific Fleet squadron to receive the F-4B Phantom. The squadron deployed twice aboard the USS Shangri-La (CVA-38) in 1958 and 1959. During the 1959 cruise VF-114 had flown 2,000 hours and had made 1,300 arrested landings without a loss of pilot or plane. In Aug. 1960 VF-114 deployed aboard the USS Hancock (CVA-19) for seven months.

Patch black and white on an orange background.

EXECUTIONER patch — red boarder, bomb-rocket and gun noses, black helmet, yellow background and silver gun-bomb-rocket.

PHOTOS: TOP — F3H-2N, 136973, on 8-57, W.T. Larkins photo. Early scheme with orange fin tip, wing tips and fuselage striping. BELOW — Two VF-114 Demons, 146739 and 146732 in flight. USN via Lt. Col. Miller. Note thin orange fin tip.

PHOTOS: TOP — Front view of F3H-2N, 136973, in the early 1957 scheme. Jannson photo. MIDDLE — 136973 again with afterburnner creating mach diamonds. Notice thin black line has been added to fin tip. USN via Wykoff. BOTTOM — F3H-2N, 137031, on 10-17-60. Note fuselage stripe is faded. Also note wing codes. USN photo.

PHOTOS: TOP — VF-114 Demons over Southern Calif. on 2-5-58. USN photo. MIDDLE — VF-114 F3H-2, 146740, refuels from A3 Skywarrior of VAH-4. USN photo. BOTTOM — VF-114 Demon, 146969, circa 1958-59 at Kadena Okinawa. Note absence of orange fin tip or fuselage stripes. Via D. Spering.

VF-121 'PACEMAKERS'

In 1958 under a reorganization plan for carrier aviation, VF-121 became the west coasts permanenet replacement Air Group. Charged with the mission of indoctrinating aviators and maintenance personnel into the fleet, VF-121 was equipped with the F11F Tiger, F3H Demon, F2H Banshee and F3D Skyknight. By 1965 the squadron was equipped only with F-4 Phantoms, which it flew until it was decommissioned in 1980.

VF-121 started out life as a NAS Los Alamitos reserve squadron VF-781 on 1 July 1946, flying the F6F Hellcat. Later the squadron transitioned to the F4U Corsair, then the F9F Panther, then the F9F Cougar, then the FJ-3 Fury and finally the F11F Tiger. VF-121 then merged with VF-124 to become the Pacific Coast Rag.

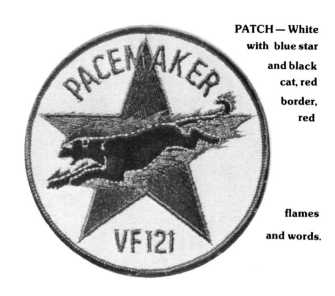

PATCH — White with blue star and black cat, red border, red flames and words.

PHOTOS: TOP — F3H-2, 145295, in grey and white scheme on 5-59, Swisher photo. Rescue arrow is yellow. BOTTOM — F3H-2, 145257, in grey and white scheme. Via W.T. Larkins.

The Skyknights of VF-121 were used to train Demon drivers in radar intercept missions, and as such were equipped with the Demons radar. The white and day-glo F3D-2T2 below was used for this purpose.

PHOTOS: TOP — F3H-2, 145256, with day-glo nose and tail. USN. MIDDLE — F3H-2, 145302, with day-glo tail and black panther on a red lightening bolt on fuselage. BOTTOM — F3H-2N, 137044, with day-glo tail and gull-grey radome. H. Gann photos.

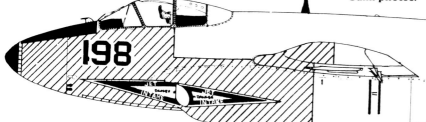

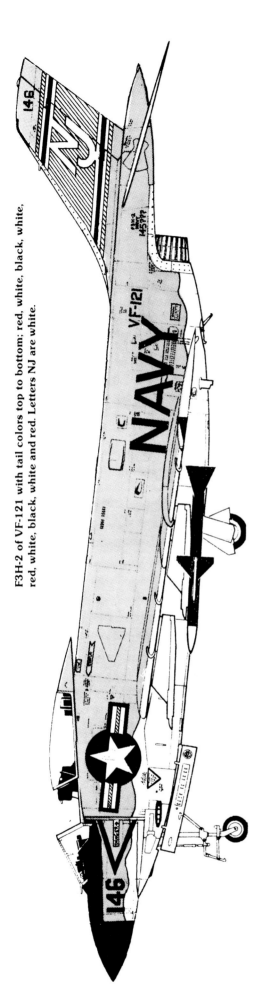

F3H-2 of VF-121 with tail colors top to bottom; red, white, black, white, red, white, black, white and red. Letters NJ are white.

AT LEFT — VF-121, F3H-2M, 137072, at Miramar on 9-12-59, Swisher photo.

AT RIGHT — VF-121, F3H-2N, 136989, in grey and white scheme with painted radome. 9-12-59 photo by Swisher.

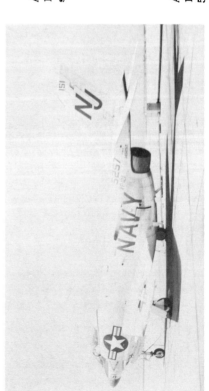

AT LEFT — VF-121, F3H-2, 145257, in grey and white scheme. Leo Kohn photo.

AT RIGHT — VF-121, 137069 at Miramar on 9-12-59, Swisher photo.

VF-122 'BLACK ANGELS'

VF-122 started out life as the 'Minute Men' of reserve squadron VF-783. The squadron was called to active duty on 20 July 1950 and became VF-122 on 4 Feb. 1953. VF-122 was then decommissioned on 1 May 1958.

The squadron received its Demons in 1957 and from 1 July to 13 July, 1957, carquals were conducted aboard the USS Kearsarge (CVA-33). Carquals were conducted twice more from 22 July to 27 July and 2 Aug. to 30 Aug. aboard the USS Ticonderoga (CVA-14). Finally on 13 Sept. 1957, VF-122 departed Alameda for a WESTPAC cruise aboard CVA-14. The cruise would prove to be a long one as the Tico would get involved with the rising tensions between the Nationalist and Red Chinese. On the 1st, 2nd, and 3rd of March, 1958, the Black Angels flew CAP sorties and on 5 March strafed a beach target. 10 March to 16 March found them covering Indonesia for possible evacuation. On 20 March CAP missions were flown in conjunction with the Chinese Nationalists.

During this cruise four Demons were lost, two fatally. LTJG Sessions died at NAS Barbers Point on 23 Sept. 1957, in F3H-2N 136986, and LTJG Witherstine lost his life at sea on 16 Nov. 1957 in F3H 160932. The two non-fatal losses of aircraft occurred at sea. F3H 136988 was lost on 30 Oct. 1957 and 136998 on 16 Nov. 1957.

PHOTOS: TOP — VF-122, F3H-2N, 137001, crash landed aboard the USS Ticonderoga (CVA-14) on 7-23-57 USN via D. Spering. Tail design is orange as well as the no. 9 and the three stripes going aft. BOTTOM — Three VF-122 Demons over Calif. with a mixed bag of armament consisting of rocket packs, practice bombs and 500 lb. bombs. National Archives photo.

Black Angel on a red background with a white boarder.

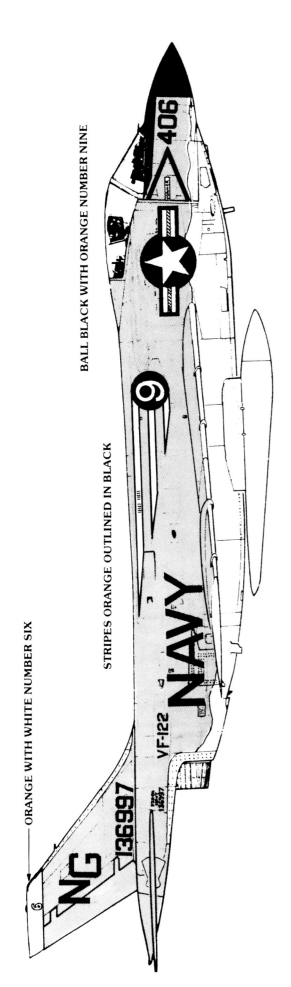

ORANGE WITH WHITE NUMBER SIX

STRIPES ORANGE OUTLINED IN BLACK

BALL BLACK WITH ORANGE NUMBER NINE

AMERICAN AVIATION
HISTORICAL SOCIETY
P. O. BOX 99,
GARDEN GROVE,
CA 92642

VF-122, F3H-2N, 136997, launches off the USS Ticonderoga on 5 Aug. 1957. National Archives photo.

VF-124 'MOONSHINERS'

VF-124 traded in their F7U's in April of 1956 and received twelve F3H-2N Demons in May, thus becoming the first Pacific coast fleet squadron to fly the type. The first four pilots worked up on the Demon with the Transitional Training Unit Pacific (TRANSTUPAC) VF(AW)3 from April to 30 June 1956. Phase I training in preparation for Lexingtons 1957 cruise started on 1 July 1956 with seventeen pilots aboard. Phase I was completed at NAS Miramar on 16 Oct. with each pilot averaging 65.8 hours. One serious and one minor accident occured during Phase I as well as one engine change because of foreign object ingestion. The more intense training Phase II started on 28 Oct. 1956 and ended on 28 Feb. 1957. During this period the aircraft on hand increased to fourteen which materially helped the squadron to attain an average of 112.2 flight hours for each pilot. Two more strikes occured during Phase II, one being fatal and one being minor. Two engines were FOD'd (foreign object damage) and had to be changed during this period. Phase III started on 28 Feb. and ended on 19 April 1957. This period was used to conduct carrier qualifications with Air Group Twelve in preparation of its April Westpac deployment of the USS Lexington (CVA-16). VF-124 completed 141 day touch and goes, 47 day bolters and 330 day traps. No accidents occured during this period, but two engines were replaced, one due to FOD and one because it was dropped.

The Lexington cruise started on 19 April 1957 and lasted until 30 Sept. 1957. The twelve aircraft deployed were BuNos 136969, 136970, 136971, 136972, 136974, 136975, 136976, 136977, 136978, 136979, 136980 and 136981. Of the twelve aircraft only ten would be aboard CVA-16 at any one time, the other two being in pool at NAS Atsugi. The statistics for the cruise minus the CAG and LSO were: hours flow, land-day 256.9, land-night 87.2, CV-day 555.4, CV-night 96.1; sorties flown, land-day 161, land-night 89, CV-day 402, CV-night 88; average aircraft availability 43.9%; CV landings, day touch and goes 102, night touch and goes 103; day bolters 18, night bolters 50, day landings 387, night landings 125; flying days, day 81, night 28; strikes 3; engine changes 4, two for high oil consumption, one bad oil seal, and one overspeed.

Prior to the cruise VF-124 was able to get the Sidewinder and gunsight cameras installed on their Demons, largely due to the efforts of Wally Schirra who had been the original Sidewinder project officer at China Lake in 1951 and 1952. VF-124 also did not utilize the in-flight refueling kits during its deployment.

After returning to NAS Miramar the squadron commenced turnabout training which ended when VF-124 merged with VF-121 and became VF-121 on 10 April 1958.

A new VF-124 was formed on 11 April 1958 and became the initial indoctrination squadron for the F-8 Crusader.

PHOTOS: TOP — F3H-2N, 133600, of VF-124 in Sept. 1956. Bowers photos via Creager. **BOTTOM —** F3H-2N, 133610, on 9-56, Bowers via Larkins. Nose gear is silver.

PHOTOS: TOP — VF-124, F3H-2N, 136972, refuels from AJ-2, 130411, OF VAH-6 on 5-9-57. USN/Tailhook photo. Tail band is yellow with two black stripes. Fuselage design is yellow with a thin black outline. MIDDLE — Sept. 1957 USN photo of three VF-124 Demons in flight. BOTTOM — Two VF-124, F3H-2N Demons, 136971 (204) and 135980 (208) off Japan. Note Sidewinders. USN/Tailhook photo.

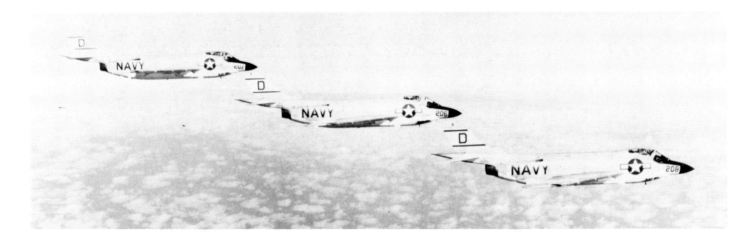

VF-131 'NIGHTCAPPERS'

BLACK WITH RED COMET

VF-131 was commissioned on 21 Aug. 1961 as part of CVG-13 for service aboard the newly commissioned USS Constellation (CVA-64). The squadron carqualed all pilots in day and night operations between 13 Jan. and 22 Jan., 1962, aboard the USS Independence (CVA-62). The squadron then went aboard their own ship (CVA-64) for a shakedown cruise to Guantonamo Bay, from 3 March until 6 May, 1962. VF-131 returned to NAS Cecil Field where on 18 May, 1962, the original CO, CDR. T. L. Johnson was relieved by CDR. Tully, but before CDR. Tully could deploy aboard the Constellation, the ship was transferred to the Pacific Fleet and VF-131 as well as other elements of CVG-13 were decommissioned in Oct. 1962.

PHOTOS: TOP — VF-131 Demon on board USS Independence (CVA-62) during Carquals in Jan. 1962. Note tail and fuselage colors have not been added yet. Photo via D. Spering. BOTTOM — F3H-2 Demons 143412 and 145242 operating off the USS Constellation (CVA-64) on 3-19-62. Note white rudder on 106 and red tail and fuselage stripe on 107. USN photo.

PHOTOS: TOP — VF-131, F3H-2, 143487, at Andrews AFB on 10 May 1962. Dave Lucabach via Jannson. Note white stars on the red tail band and the squadron patch on the red fuselage stripe. ABOVE LEFT — The end at NAF Litchfield Park on 3-18-63. Swisher photo. ABOVE RIGHT — VF-131, F3H-2, 133563, awaits the torch on 3-18-63 also. BOTTOM — VF-131, F3H-2, 136996, in the sun at NAS Cecil Field Fla. Note open armament door and missile computer hanging out the bottom of the nose wheel well. Photo via D. Spering.

VF-141 "IRON ANGELS"

VF-141 turned in their F2H-3 Banshees in June 1956 for the Douglas F4D-1 Skyray. The Ford was flown till July 27, 1959 when the squadron re-equipped with F3H Demons.

From its base at NAS Miramar, the squadron spent Oct. 1st to 9th and Nov. 2nd to 6th aboard the USS Oriskany (CVA-34). The squadron CO, CDR. Tuttle, made his 600th carrier landing and CVA-34's 41,000th landing on 7 Oct. 1959.

During the first few months of 1960, VF-141 went aboard the Oriskany on Feb. 15th to 19th and March 7th to 11th. Finally on 8 April 1960, the "Iron Angels" deployed on CVA-34 until 15 Dec. During this cruise VF-141 participated in operations "Slo Gin", "Square Knot" and "Checkertail". While in West Pac, LTJG. Henry made the 44,000th Oriskany landing and thirteen VF-141 pilots became Centurians on the cruise. In addition, CDR. Tuttle became a Oriskany Centurian on 22 Sept. 1960.

1961 brought about the replacement of all but four of the squadron's pilots, which of course brought about a complete training syllabus. Initial carrier qualifications occurred aboard CVA-34 between 27 Feb. to 3 March 1961, and between 12 March and 31 March the squadron deployed to MCAAS Yuma for night ground control intercept training and night field carrier mirror landing practice. While back at NAS Miramar, the squadron won the AIRPAC battle efficiency "E" and took part in the Sidewinder missile firing exercise of Aug. 25th. The squadron embarked on the USS Lexington (CVA-16) for night carrier qualification on the 10th to the 22nd of July and the 11th to the 22nd of Sept. 1961. On 9 Nov. 1961, VF-141 left on its last Demon deployment, which lasted until June of 1962. When the squadron returned to NAS Miramar, it traded its Demons for the F8U-2NE Crusader.

PHOTO BELOW — Two VF-141 Demons, 1333594 and 133604, in flight on 2-13-61. Fin-tip is red with a small bottom black boarder. Note both planes have the long beaver tail. USN photo by Batzler.

PATCH — Red boarder and wording IRON ANGELS; yellow halo, wings, bullets, handles and background for words; white cloud; light grey background; dark grey knight and gun.

PHOTO BELOW — VF-141 F3H-2, 133579, on 3-18-63 at NAF Litchfield Park. Note "E" on shield behind refueling probe, fin-tip is red with black bottom boarder and styleized yellow birds, also note non-standard white rudder. Swisher photo.

PHOTO ABOVE — VF-141, F3H-2, 146717, lands on the USS Oriskany (CVA-34) on 10-59. USN/Tailhook photo. BELOW — 133556 with red fin tip at Litchfield Park on 3-18-63. Via Jannson.

Fighter Squadron One Fifty One was originally commissioned as VF-23 in 1948 at NAS Oceana flying the F4U Corsair. VF-23 would go on to fly the F9F Panther, the F2H Banshee and the F4D Skyray before acquiring the F3H Demon and their new designation of VF-151 in Feb. of 1959. In early 1964 the squadron transitioned to the F-4 Phantom and today flies the F-14 Tomcat.

While flying the Demon VF-151 deployed once aboard the USS Hancock (CVA-19) in 1959 and three times aboard the USS Coral Sea (CVA-43) in 1961 and in 1963 as part of CVG-15.

HARRY MILNER REMEMBERS VF-151

As a point of interest, Harry Milner had this to say about VF-151: "While on cruise we added red rotating beacons to the top of our rudders. Since this was an on going project, we had some with and some without. The brief was that if you had it, you had to have it turned on. Of course nobody did this, they just waited out there at night for another red beacon to come along and then bounce them."

VF-151 'VIGILANTES'

Black background, red boarder, red VF-151, red eyes, red flame or knife, yellow nutron tracks, lt. grey skull and knife handle, white knife blade.

PHOTOS: TOP — VF-151, F3H-2, 136985, on 5-60, fin tip is red. MIDDLE — 145267 also on 5-60, note Sparrow III missiles. Photos via W.T. Larkins. BOTTOM — 145252 and 143408 in flight, USN photo. 143408 has USS Coral Sea painted on tail and a red styleized boar on the fuselage.

PHOTO ABOVE — Coral Sea Air Group 15 in the air. VAH-4 Skywarrier, VF-151 F3H, VA-155 and VA-153 Skyhawks, VA-152 Skyraider and VF-154 Crusader. USN via Wyckoff. BELOW — Close up of nose of VF-151 Demon on the Coral Sea (CVA-43) on 3-14-61. Note open gun door. USN photo.

PHOTOS: TOP — VF-151 F3H, 146724, at NAS Lemoore on 7-8-61. Swisher photo. AT RIGHT — 133594 with Sidewinder and one belly tank. BOTTOM — VF-151 F3H-2, 146734, being started on the Cat aboard the Coral Sea (CVA-43) on 3-1-61. USN photo.

VF-151 'VIGILANTES'

PHOTOS: TOP — VF-151, Demons 133594 and 146734, off CVA-43 over the Western Pacific. Note they are dumping fuel. MIDDLE — VF-151, F3H-2, 146724, being launched from CVA-43 while moored at Yokosuka Japan on 3-13-62. BOTTOM — Three F3H aircraft of VF-151, 145252, 133594, 133550, with two VF-154 Crusaders in trail. Note Delmar tow target being carried by the last Demon. USN photos.

PHOTOS: TOP — VF-151, F3B, 146719, in flight rudder stripes are red and white with white VF-151 emblems on fin. ABOVE — F3B, 146735, at NAS Agana Guam on 5-21-63. USN photos. Note small kangaroo on the nose. AT RIGHT — Pilots of VF-151 on 6-14-63, via H. Miller. BELOW — F3H-2, 145209, on 1-63. Jannson photo.

VF-161 'CHARGERS'

Fighter Squadron One Hundred Sixty One was recommissioned on 1 Sept. 1960 at NAS Cecil Field as part of CVG-16. The squadron and the air group were transferred to the Pacific Fleet at NAS Miramar in Sept. 1961. The Chargers deployed twice aboard the USS Oriskany (CVA-34) in 1962 and in 1963. The squadron transitioned to the F-4 Phantom on 21 Sept. 1964, marking the end of the Demons nine year career which saw 519 F3H's delivered to the fleet. An interesting fact is that the Demon disappeared quickly from its desert retirement with only two left in 1967.

VF-161 was originally commissioned during World War II flying from the decks of the USS Lexington and the USS Randolph. The squadron was then decommissioned in 1945 after hostilitites ceased.

HARRY MILER REMEMBERS VF-161

LT. Harry Miler was the OPS officer of VF-161 when the Demon was retired in 1964. He was the officer who held the personnel inspection during the retirement ceremony. The CO, CDR. Welty, and the XO, LCDR. Baldridge, took the two Demons to Litchfield Park on thier last flight. The squadrons first F-4B had been delivered that same day by CAPT. Pat Murphy. The squadron then went through conversion training with VF-121.

PHOTO ABOVE — Black and white shield with red chevrons, background and writing.

PHOTOS: TOP — VF-161, F3B, 145259, via W.T. Larkins. Check marks and fin tip are red. Note shield at top of rudder. **BELOW** — F3B, 145266 in same markings. H. Gann photo.

PHOTOS: TOP — VF-161, F3H, 145295, lands on the USS Kitty Hawk (CVA-63) on 11-13-61. USN photo. Name behind star is LT. JG GALLAGHER USN. BOTTOM — VF-161, F3H, ready to launch from the USS Oriskany (CVA-34). USN photo.

PHOTOS: TOP — Jannson photo of VF-161 Demons 143421 and 145222 in flight. MIDDLE — USN photo via Milner of 145266, 145259, 145248 and 145295 of VF-161 in flight. BOTTOM — VF-161, F3B, 145266, kicks in afterburner prior to evening launch from the USS Oriskany (CVA-34). Note squadron badge in front of red fuselage chevron. USN photo.

Overhead view of four VF-161 Demons, USN photo via Harry Milner.

PHOTO ABOVE — Last of the Fleet's Demons, F3B, 145295, is piped over the side, at NAS Miramar, Calif. The last flight was piloted by CDR Wayne Welty, CO of VF-161 on 9-21-64. USN photo.

VF-193 'GHOST RIDERS'

Originally commissioned at NAS Alameda as VF-193 in 1948 flying the F8F Bearcat, the Ghostriders transitioned to the F4U Corsair in 1950, and completed two combat deployments during the Korean War. In 1952 with Air Group Nineteen at NAS Moffett Field, the squadron transitioned to the jet age flying the F2H-3 Banshee. From 1957 to 1963 VF-193 operated the F3H Demon. In 1963, the Demon was replaced by the F4B Phantom and the squadrons designation changed to VF-142. In 1974 the squadron transitioned to the F-14 Tomcat which it flies today.

While flying the Demon, VF-193 won three Aviation Safety Awards in 1958, 1959 and 1962. VF-193 would also take the F3H on four cruises aboard the USS Bon Homme Richard (CVA-31). The deployments were from Nov. 1958 until June 1959, Nov. 1959 until May 1960, April 1961 until Dec. 1961 and July 1962 until Feb. 1963. On the third cruise LCDR. W. McLuckie, XO of VF-193 made the 69,000th landing aboard CVA-31. Two other note worthy events took place on the fourth cruise. VF-193's LCDR. D. E. Swank made the 86,000th landing and a Ghostrider Demon was honored with the ships 40,000th accident free Cat shot.

Black horse white robes & scroll on a yellow diamond or black horse red robes and scroll on a blue diamond.

PHOTOS: TOP — VF-193, F3H-2, 143440, on 5-58 at NAS Moffett Field, W.T. Larkins photo. Fuselage design and tail diamond are blue with a thin white outline. Note Silhouette of F11F above star, pilots name is LCDR E. I. Whitlock. MIDDLE — Two F3H-2 Demons of VF-193, 145232 and 133593 in 1958. Fin tips and blue, note wing codes. USN/Tailhook photo. BOTTOM — Two VF-193 Demons, 145229 and 145228, on 6-29-59. MDC photo.

First two photos in a series of a VF-193 F3B, 143457, making a first recovery attempt. USN photos. barrier landing because the aircrafts starboard strut broke during its

PHOTOS: TOP — VF-193, F3B, 143457, takes the barrier, note the odd angle of the broken starboard gear. Note fin tip and tail markings as well as fuselage markings are blue. MIDDLE — 143457 finally stop, note battle "E" on intake. 2-10-63 USN photos. BOTTOM — 5-2-59 photo of CVA-31 and Air Group 19 off Japan. F3H, F11F, FJ4-B, A1 and A3s.

VF-213 'BLACK LIONS'

The 'Black Lions' transitioned to the F4D-1 Skyray from the F2H-3 Banshee in Feb. 1957. The Fords in turn were replaced by F3H Demons on 14 Dec. 1959.

The squadron and its Demons were home ported at NAS Moffett Field and flew from the USS Hancock (CVA-19) from 21 March to 24 March 1960. On the day of the squadrons return to Moffett, the CO, CDR. Thompson was killed while doing an instrument approach to NAS Moffett Field. Following this accident the squadron deployed to NAAS Fallon, Nevada from 11 April until 24 April, and simultaneously worked out of NAS Pt. Mugu from 18 April until 22 April, 1960. VF-213 then spent 2 May to 6 May aboard CVA-19 and 20 June to 2 July aboard the USS Lexington (CVA-16). After more time at NAS Pt. Mugu the squadron returned aboard CVA-16 from 15-26 Aug, 8-12 Sept. and 1-13 Oct. 1960. During this period of time, the squadron also received the COMNAVAIR-PAC Safety Award and became the first F3H unit to supply its own target tow service, using the Delmar device.

Finally the squadron deployed on CVA-16 from 28 Oct. 1960 to 5 June 1961. During this cruise, the squadron participated in three major operations. The first was WEPTRAEX 3-60 and exercise Steeple-Jack. This was the first major Fleet strike and weapons training exercise and VF-213 was responsible for around-the-clock Combat Air Patrol. The second operation was the Seventh Fleet firepower demonstration for SEATO Military leaders on 6-9 Feb. 1961. The third operation, 'Grass Shack', took place on 3 June 1961. VF-213 was detailed to penetrate the NORAD coastal defences. The squadron was also trained in firing the Sparrow III missile on 13 March 1961 by Utility Squadron 5, Okinawa.

After the Lexington returned home, VF-213 participated in the opening ceremonies of NAS Lemoore, Calif., on 8 July 1961. 12 July would find the 'Black Lions' at their new home, NAS Miramar. Since its relocation, the squadron engaged in a training cycle which encompassed three short carrier qualification deployments aboard the USS Coral Sea (CVA-43), USS Oriskany (CVA-34), USS Hancock (CVA-19) and extensive training in day and night fighter tactics.

On 2 Feb. 1962, VF-213 deployed aboard CVA-19 on a WEST PAC cruise which ended on 20 Oct. 1962. During this cruise VF-213 operated as both defender and aggressor for operation 'Tulungun', the largest amphibious exercise since World War II. Four other operations during this period were, 'Newboy', 'Sea Dev il', and 'Checkertail #1 and #2'. By June 1962, all squadron pilots qualified as 'Centurions' with 100 arrested landings aboard Hancock.

Fighter Squadron 213 was the first carrier based squadron in the Pacific Fleet to furnish Del Mar Aerial towed Target services for radar intercept and missile firing practice by fighter aircraft of the British Royal Navy in addition to providing their own target service and that for ships gunnery practice. On 6 May 1962 LT. D.A. Pedersen towed the Del Mar for Sea Vixens of the 890 squadron from the HMS Ark Royal. On 20 June Capt. Eager, USAF exchange pilot, towed Firestreak missile practic by the 800 squadron Scimitars during joint operations aboard the HMS Ark Royal. After the Ark Royal operations, two other events took place, they were 'Grass Shack VII' and 'ky Shield III'.

In preparation for their third cruise VF-213 conducted six short training missions aboard Hancock. These were from 5 Nov. 1962 to 8 Nov., 13 Feb. 1963 to 15 Feb., 11 March to 2 April, 17 April to 26 April and 16 May to 21 May. They finally deployed on CVA-19 from 7 June 1963 to 15 Dec. 1963. During Nov. VF-213 participated in an emergency sortie from Hong Kong to support possible evacuation of United States citizens from Saigon, Republic of Vietnam. This was the second demonstration of the Attack Carrier's flexibility and mobility in rendering assistance during the Vietnam crisis.

Upon return to NAS Miramar on 16 Dec. 1963, VF-213 began working up for its transition to the F4B Phantom in March 1964.

PHOTO BELOW — VF-213, F3H-2, 146737, on board ship on 8-19-61. Swisher photo. Fin tip powder blue.

PHOTOS: TOP — F3H of VF-213 catapulted from the USS Lexington (CVA-16). MIDDLE — VF-213, F3B, 145270, at NAS Miramar on 1-19-63, lion is black, fin tip is powder blue with yellow stars. Jannson photo. BELOW — VF-213, F3H-2, 146739, on 9-62. W.T. Larkins photo.

PHOTOS: TOP — VF-213, F3B, 133467 and 133471 launch off the USS Hancock (CVA-19) off Calif. in May 1963. Note pilots name on anti-glare panels and unusual shape of wing-walks. BELOW — 145270 follows two A4 Skyhawks.

ALMOST A PHANTOM THE F3H-G/H PROPOSAL

George Watkins had this to say of the F3H. 'Perhaps the greatest contribution that the Demon made to military aviation, was that it enabled the McDonnell Aircraft Co. to build an outstanding follow-on airplane, drawing heavily from the mistakes made in the design technology of the F3H, and retaining, wisely, the very satisfactory flying qualitites that the Demon had. that plane was the F4H Phantom II.'

What follows are excerpts from the F3H-G/H design proposal showing the emergence of the budding F4H design. The difference between the F3H-G and the F3H-H is that the G version was to be equipped with two J-65 engines and the H was to have two J-79 engines. Before the F3H-G/H proposal a F3H-C and a F3H-E were proposed. The C was basically a regular F3H-2 fitted with a single J-67 engine. The E also was to have the J-67 engine, but the airframe was to have a different wing, similar to that of the F3H-G/H and a fuselage similar to the F11F.

PHOTO BELOW — F3H-G/H mock-up at St. Louis in May 1954, MDC photo. Note the basic phantom lines. Bend the outer wings up and the tailplanes down and whala a single seat Phantom.

COMPARISONS

MODEL	F3H-2	F3H-C	F3H-E	F3H-G	F3H-H
ENGINE(S)	J-71	J-67	J-67	Two J-65s	Two J-79s
THRUST	11,000	13,200	13,200	7,600	9,292
AFTERBURNER	15,500	21,500	21,500	11,000	14,346
WING AREA, SQ. FT.	442	458	450	530	530
WING SPAN, FT.	35.33	36.3	36.75	38.6	38.6
WING SWEEP, DEG.	45°	45°	45°	45°	45°
WING CHORD	8.6/6.4	8.6/6.4	5.0	5.0	5.0
LENGTH, FT.	59.45	59.1	56	56	56
MAX. SPEED AT SEA LEVEL KTS.	636	692	700	661	661
MACH	.962	1.05	1.06	1.00	1.00
MAX. 35,000 FT. KTS.	568	860	973	875	1,133
MACH	.988	1.49	1.69	1.52	1.97
MAX. 45,000 FT. KTS.	551	780	920	805	1,081
MACH	.958	1.36	1.60	1.40	1.88
RATE OF CLIMB, FPM	19,180	34,250	37,200	32,800	44,100
COMBAT CEILING, FT.	49,690	55,150	55,450	55,500	59,200

PHOTO — F3H-G/H mock-up at St. Louis in May 1954. MDC photo.

F3H-G EXTERNAL STORES CARRYING CAPABILITY CHART

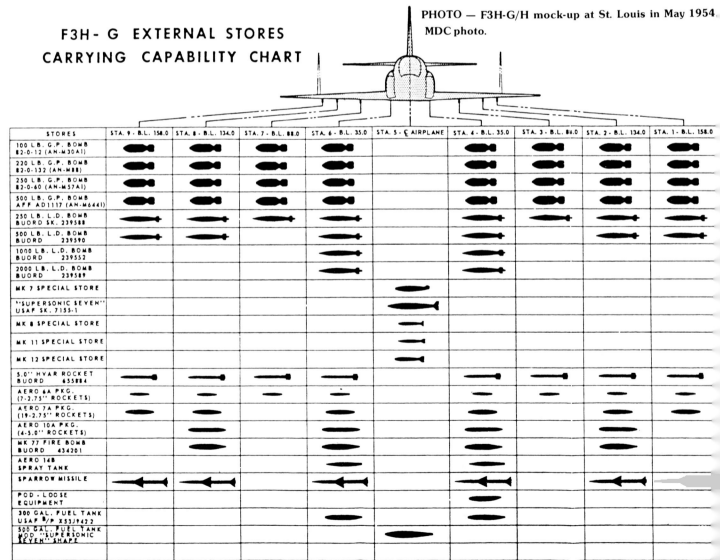

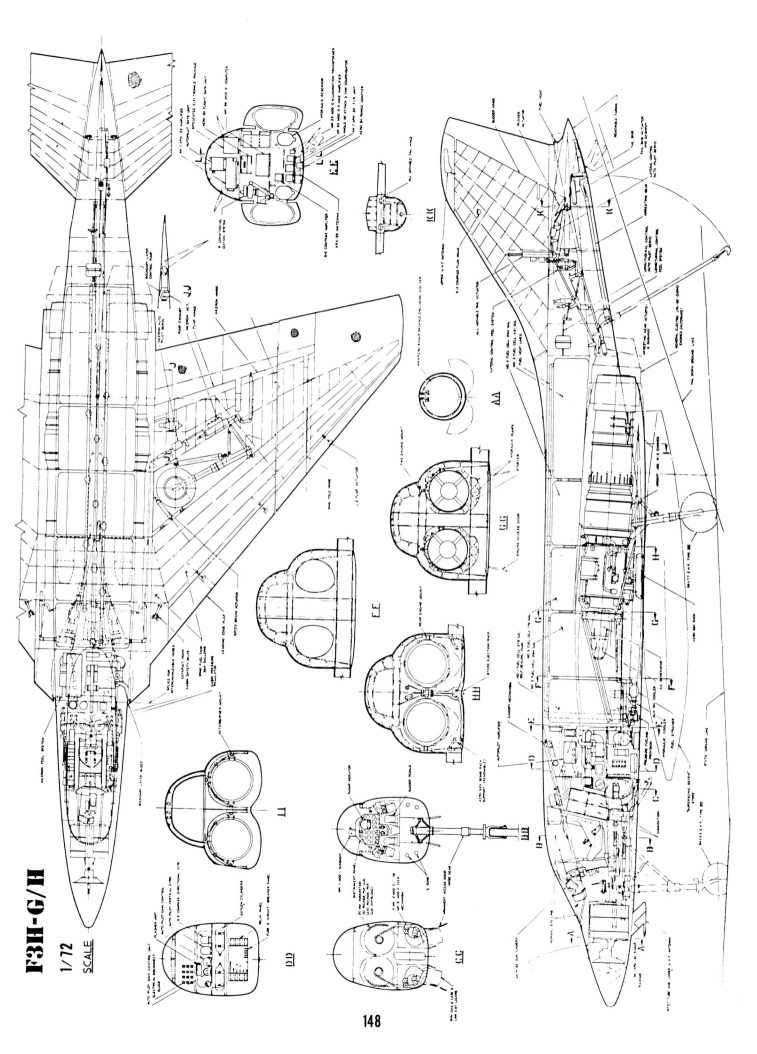

F3H - G
NOSE ASSEMBLY ATTACHMENT

THE INTERCHANGEABLE NOSE ASSEMBLY IS ATTACHED TO THE AIRFRAME WITH APPROXIMATELY 30 BOLTS. IT IS ESTIMATED THAT 4 MEN COULD CHANGE NOSE ASSEMBLIES WITHIN 8 HOURS ABOARD A CARRIER OR AT AN ADVANCED BASE.

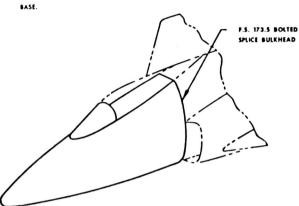

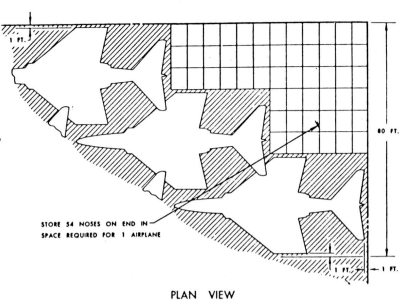

PLAN VIEW

STOWAGE

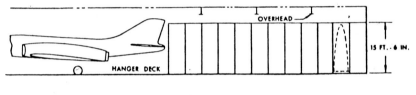

SHEER VIEW

Included in the F3H-G/H proposal was the old Douglas F3D Skyknight idea of interchangeable nose assemblies for greater versatility.

MACH LIMITATIONS WITH STORES

CONFIGURATION	F3H-G	F3H-H
TWO 300 GALLLON TANKS	1.17	1.57
ONE 'SUPERSONIC SEVEN' STORE	1.27	1.68
MK 7 STORE	1.25	1.64
FOUR SPARROWS	1.37	1.77
SIX SPARROWS	1.30	1.68

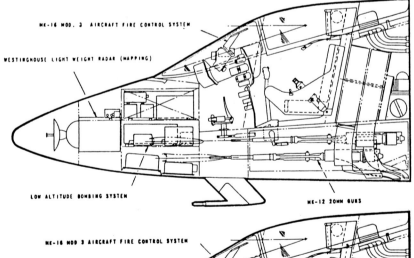

F3H-G   JET ATTACK

JET ATTACK - Incorporates the basic four 20mm guns and provisions for external stores with simplified search and mapping equipment for accurate attack. A radar ranging feature for defensive air-to-air combat is included. The following may be incorporated in place of the four 20mm guns:
1) 56 two-inch FFAR on retractible racks
2) Two 20mm guns plus IFR probe
3) 28 two-inch FFAR plus IFR probe

F3H-G   ALL-WEATHER ATTACK FIGHTER

This airplane incorporates APQ-50 radar for search, track and fire control and four MK-12 20mm guns and 600 rounds of ammunition for a high performance fighter configuration. Addition of nine store racks completes the attack version, permitting the delivery of a multiple combination of stores and special weapons at distant targets through inclement weather from ship or shore.